POW 1971

POW 1971

A Soldier's Account
of the Battle of Daruchhian

Major General Vijay Singh

SPEAKING TIGER BOOKS LLP
125A, Ground Floor, Shahpur Jat, near Asiad Village,
New Delhi 110049

Published by Speaking Tiger Books 2021

Copyright © Vijay Singh 2021

ISBN: 978-93-5447-027-1
eISBN: 978-93-5447-019-6

All photographs courtesy of the author unless specified otherwise.

10 9 8 7 6 5 4 3 2 1

All rights reserved.
No part of this publication may be reproduced, transmitted, or
stored in a retrieval system, in any form or by any means, electronic,
mechanical, photocopying, recording or otherwise,
without the prior permission of the publisher.

This book is sold subject to the condition that it shall not, by way of
trade or otherwise, be lent, resold, hired out, or otherwise circulated,
without the publisher's prior consent, in any form of binding
or cover other than that in which it is published.

*To my loving parents
whose life has been far from ordinary.
You faced your challenges alone,
shielding us from your trials and tribulations.
We will need many more lifetimes
to reciprocate our gratitude.*

Brigadier Hamir Singh with his two sons, Vikram and Vijay, both serving Major Generals in the army, in front of a portrait of Major General Kalyan Singh.

Major Hamir Singh.

CONTENTS

Preface   xi

Prologue   1
Part One: The Battle   3
Part Two: The Road to Recovery   75
Part Three: POW Camp, Lyallpur   153
Part Four: Homecoming   187
Epilogue   212
Postscript   219

Glossary and Explanations   227
Notes   232
Acknowledgments   237

Preface

Every war has its winners and losers, heroes and cowards, living and dead, some remembered and some forgotten. But behind each person is a family that carries their legacy.

When the dust settles after the war, memories tend to fade, especially if the battle isn't won. The generations that follow are then left with very little information to refer to—a citation for the fortunate few who were conferred awards for gallantry, while for the others, an odd mention in historical books or regimental folklore.

My father was among the fortunate few whose courage during the 1971 war between India and Pakistan was recognized. He was awarded a Vir Chakra for the part he played in the Battle of Daruchhian[1] in Jammu and Kashmir.

His citation reads:

> On the night of 13/14 December 1971, Captain Hamir Singh was commanding a company of Grenadiers during the attack on Daruchhian in the Western Sector. His Company was given the task to capture West Spur of the objective. He moved his Company deep in enemy territory and attacked the objective. The enemy was taken by surprise and the objective fell. He moved forward with his men to take some more positions of the objective, but he came under heavy automatic fire from enemy bunkers and pillboxes. Undeterred, he pressed on and captured some more positions of the objective. When his men could not move any further he quickly ordered them to prepare themselves for the inevitable counterattacks of the enemy during the day. The enemy reacted faster than expected and launched a series of counterattacks but he successfully repulsed the

counterattacks. Despite several severe bullet injuries in his arm and chest, he remained calm and displayed cool courage under adverse circumstances and under heavy automatic and artillery fire. When his strength was diminishing rapidly, an airstrike was arranged to silence the most dangerously sighted pillbox. When the pillbox was struck by the aircraft he quickly charged the enemy bunker with his Company Headquarter personnel and artillery observation officer's party. By his personal courage and tenacity he infused in his men the determination to hold on to the objective in spite of depleted strength and under heavy enemy fire. In this action, Captain Hamir Singh displayed gallantry and determination of a high order.[2]

It was nearly fifty years ago that my father and his colleagues participated in this furious battle on the slopes of Daruchhian. What transpired during the battle and how gallantly the men fought run the risk of being remembered in future through just these 252 words that make up his citation.

The attack on Daruchhian was a failure.

But the failure does not take away from the valour of the eight officers, seven JCOs (junior commissioned officers) and 149 men of other ranks of 14 Grenadiers who were killed, injured or went missing[3] in this battle. 'There were many a gallant deed by Major H.S. Chahal, M.H. Khan, Hamir Singh and Subedar Taj Mohammad, among others who went unrewarded. Two VrCs [Vir Chakras] were, however, awarded much later,'[4] records Lieutenant Colonel (Retd) Gautam Sharma.

While Major M.H. Khan was awarded his VrC during the war the two recipients of the VrC awarded 'much later', in January 1973, were my father Major Hamir Singh and his forward observation officer (FOO) Captain J.C. Gosain[5] of 196 Mountain Regiment. Hidden amidst their citations lies a saga of bravery, sacrifice and devotion to duty by a large number of soldiers whom not many have heard of or remember.

While I have tried to imagine the conversations that took place, adding a few details where gaps remained, each incident mentioned was experienced by my father and the book is

Preface

Hamir Singh (seated, extreme left) with the men of 14 Grenadiers. This is one of the few photos he has with the men of his battalion as he had left shortly after this for Nigeria and returned just prior to the war.

Hamir Singh (seated, extreme left) with the men of his battalion.

based on his personal notes penned down immediately after the war and his narration of the events to us.

I write this story on behalf of my father, to honour the martyrs of 14 Grenadiers and other units supporting them who died fighting in the Battle of Daruchhian.

May their legacy never fade into the sands of time!

Prologue

14 December 1971. On the Slopes of Daruchhian

'Sahab...sahab ji...'

The voice was weak, almost faint and in some distress. The words, however, sounded familiar. They could have been spoken either by one of his men, who referred to my father Major Hamir Singh as sahab (pronounced 'saab') or my mother, Laxmi, who fondly called him 'Saabji'.

Whether it was the voice of one of his men or Laxmi didn't really matter. He loved them both equally and, therefore, the words demanded his immediate attention.

'Haan, kaun?' he muttered, opening his eyes. *Who is it?* He glanced in the direction of the source of the sound—whether it was the voice of a man or a woman, strangely, he doesn't remember.

To his surprise there was no one to be seen. But then the voice had been very real. He was now a bit confused; to make matters worse he had no recollection of where he was. It was mid morning and he could feel the warmth of the morning sun. But what was he doing lying out in the open, tucked uncomfortably amid a pair of large boulders?

He glanced to his left and then to his right. Not finding anyone or anything familiar, he turned his head to look behind him. He was stunned by what he saw. The body of a soldier lay in a bizarre position, a position possible only in death.

The shock of seeing his dead colleague instantly brought him back to reality—he had been knocked down by the blast of a near-miss artillery shell. His objective, Daruchhian Top, was still about 150 yards away. As he contemplated his next move his father's words echoed in his head—'Son, I can bear your loss, but not disgrace!'

Under intense enemy fire, Hamir stood up, adjusting his heavily bandaged right arm into its sling over his damp blood-soaked shirt. Seeing him get back on his feet, his men followed, standing abreast, rifles in their hands. Hamir hung his personal weapon on his back. It was of little use now; he had lost the use of his firing arm. *I am afraid you will have to live with my loss, Papa.* 'Sarvada Shaktishali,' he yelled, and was off, leading his band of thirty-odd soldiers to their destiny, as the enemy beckoned from Daruchhian Top.

Part One
THE BATTLE

7 November 1971

War with Pakistan seemed imminent. Preparations were in full swing all along the western front. Major General Kundan Singh, General Officer Commanding (GOC) 25 Infantry Division was on a visit to 120 Infantry Brigade to review plans.

25 Infantry Division was responsible for the defence of approximately 180 kilometres of Indian Territory along the Ceasefire Line (CFL, now referred to as LOC) with Pakistan in the state of Jammu and Kashmir. 14 Grenadiers was one of the infantry battalions which formed part of 120 Infantry Brigade of the division.

Lieutenant Colonel Inderjit Singh, OC, 14 Grenadiers had just completed presenting his attack plan to Maj Gen Kundan Singh, who had been his instructor at the Senior Command Course at the Army War College.[6]

'You need to reconsider this plan, Inderjit! It is too complicated and providing artillery support for the attack will be a challenge,' Kundan Singh warned. 'Don't you remember what I taught you during the Senior Command Course? Plans must be simple and practical,' he remarked, somewhat irritated by the impracticability of the plan. 'Go for it *only* if you can sell it to your Commander!' he added, glancing at Brigadier Hari Singh, commander of the 120 Infantry Brigade.

Inderjit was upset by the abject rejection of his attack plan. To make matters worse his professional ego had been hurt in the presence of a room full of colleagues. Inderjit left the operations room in a huff.

~

Lt Col Inderjit had taken over command of 14 Grenadiers in November 1970 as it moved to Rajouri. The battalion was tasked to defend an area of approximately eighteen kilometres of the Mendhar Sector. The area in its charge being large, each of its four rifle companies had been further split into platoons to ensure physical presence throughout its defensive responsibility. The battalion remained deployed in such a dispersed manner until June '71, when it was assigned a new task. It was now earmarked as the reserve battalion of 25 Infantry Division.

Being a reserve battalion meant that it would no longer be occupying defensive positions. Instead, it would be so located that it could be employed anywhere within the 180 kilometres of the divisional sector.

Accordingly, 14 Grenadiers relocated to Sarol, near Rajouri, to prepare for its new task. It had been assigned many possible areas where the battalion could be employed. This meant a lot of hard work as the battalion had now to do extensive reconnaissance and coordination throughout the 180-kilometre frontage of the division.

On 3 December 1971 Pakistan Air Force launched pre-emptive strikes on airfields in western India. India responded by formally declaring war on Pakistan in the wee hours of the fourth of December.

By this time 14 Grenadiers was fully prepared to take on any of its assigned tasks as the reserve battalion.

However, they were in for a surprise!

9 December 1971

In a surprising development, Brigadier Hari Singh received orders to launch 14 Grenadiers for an attack. The objective was Daruchhian, a steep hill held by the enemy and the attack was to be launched just four days later on 13 December.

An attack on Daruchhian had been anticipated. Accordingly, the task had been assigned to 6/11 GR (6th Battalion of the 11 Gorkha Rifles), the other infantry battalion of the brigade and it had prepared for it. The division was aware of this, therefore the order to employ 14 Grenadiers for the attack on

Daruchhian was surprising and unusual. Brigadier Hari Singh was a bit upset by this change.

At the time of receiving the fresh orders 14 Grenadiers were spread out in company groups in accordance with their tasks as reserve battalion. Alpha Company was at Bhimber Gali[7] for purposes of patrolling. Bravo and Charlie Company were at Poonch to strengthen the defences, while Delta Company was deployed to assist in the defence of Pir Badesar.[8]

Normally, prior to launching a battalion for an attack it is allowed at least a couple of nights to prepare. This time is required for it to carry out reconnaissance, rehearsals and other preparations essential for the attack. Dispersed as the battalion was 14 Grenadiers would find it difficult to even reach the area. There would be hardly any time available for reconnaissance and other preparatory activities prior to the offensive being launched on 13 December.

To make matters worse Lt Col Inderjit had a superstitious fear of the number 13, which he considered unlucky. Given the short notice, change of task and his superstition, Inderjit had requested for a delay of at least one day. Hari Singh, however, had not been able to accede to his request as the Corps HQ had declined a postponement.[9]

A conference was held at Brigade HQ the next day to finalize the modalities of the attack. When they met, Hari Singh realized that Inderjit was already under tremendous pressure. Therefore he decided against encumbering him any further by forcing a plan on him.

'Inder, I don't want to tie you down with the plan of 6/11 GR, who were initially tasked for Daruchhian. Please feel free to make your own plan,' Hari Singh remarked.

'Thank you sir, I appreciate that,' Inderjit replied.

'Just one suggestion though. Do keep in mind General Kundan Singh's comments on your plan. He's an experienced soldier; I suggest you follow the advice he gave you in November.'

Inderjit nodded, saluted smartly and walked away to his jeep. He had no intentions of changing his unconventional plan. He had deliberated over it several times and even rehearsed his battalion for it while training in June. He was confident of its success. Besides, in his mind he had the 'tacit approval'[10] of the GOC.

Unconventional plans, since they tend to involve a high degree of risk, can very easily turn into catastrophic failure during execution. But when successful they bring great glory. The order for the attack on Daruchhian by his battalion was just the opportunity he had been looking for—the opportunity to redeem his plan and professional honour.

~

The objective for the attack, Daruchhian, is an innocuous hill located along the Ceasefire Line between Poonch and Mendhar.[11] A cone-shaped feature, approximately 1,000 metres in height, it is narrow on the top with precipitous projections. The feature was covered with forests on all sides, except for the south-western slopes, which lacked tree cover. However, these slopes had a scattered growth of low scrub.

The Pakistani strength at Daruchhian was assessed to be not more than two platoons.[12] These troops were supported by the nearby Pakistani pickets—'Three Star' in the north and 'Black Rock' in the south.

Daruchhian's relative position amidst the neighbouring area gave it considerable tactical significance. It was appreciated that the capture of this feature would lead to the fall of Three Star.

In addition Daruchhian commanded the strategically important road connecting the Pakistani towns of Kotli and Hajira. This road followed the eastern bank of the Poonch River and skirted the base of Daruchhian from the west, passing through a small village called Sehra. The village had been abandoned due to the impending war.

From Sehra the road continued northwards until it reached the point where the Mendhar River joined the Poonch River north of Daruchhian. A bridge (Mendhar Bridge) had been constructed on the Mendhar River to facilitate movement of vehicles across the river to Hajira.

A number of nalas originating from the surrounding mountains flowed downstream into the Poonch and Mendhar rivers. One such fast-flowing nala ran along the southern slopes of Daruchhian. The Kotli–Hajira road crossed this nala over a bridge, just south of Sehra village.

All this meant that Daruchhian was a military objective of great significance. Therefore, in planning its capture the GOC had made a sound tactical decision.

His decision, however, to employ 14 Grenadiers for the attack on Daruchhian was unusual, given that 6/11 GR had already been given this task prior to the war.

~

From the standpoint of the Pakistanis the tactical importance of Daruchhian meant that it had to be well defended and protected. Accordingly the Pakistanis were well entrenched on Daruchhian and had spared no effort in their preparations to take on an Indian attack. They would react violently to any assault.

Defending a mountain primarily involves denying access to its top or apex. Once the top is captured the attacker could literally roll down in any direction, rendering defences on all other parts of the mountain vulnerable.

To reach the apex of the mountain the attacker is required to climb up the tongues of land connecting its top to the valley below. In military parlance these are referred to as 'spurs' and provide the easier routes to the top of the mountain. For planning purposes spurs are normally given names based on their geographical direction.

Spurs are defended to prevent an attacker reaching the top directly. Therefore to reach the top of the mountain an attacker would have to fight the defended positions located on the spurs leading to it. Defences on spurs would normally consist of pillboxes and bunkers sited behind natural rocks.

Daruchhian Top was a narrow rocky ledge right at the very top of the mountain. Top provided good observation in all directions. Therefore the Pakistanis had constructed strong concrete bunkers on the Top from where their medium (MMG) and heavy machine guns (HMG) could effectively target attackers from any direction.

The Indian defensive position opposite Daruchhian was the picket Point 471, located on its east. To attack Daruchhian one would need to descend from Point 471 to the geographical saddle situated right on the Ceasefire Line. This saddle, referred to as Neck, connected Point 471 to Daruchhian. From Neck, to reach Top one would need to climb up the eastern spur of Daruchhian.

The Pakistani position on Daruchhian's eastern spur was called OP Position. Being the easiest and, therefore, the most obvious approach to Top, OP Position was well prepared to take on an attack.

The south-western slopes of Daruchhian were defended by Pakistani troops occupying a position called South West (SW) Spur.

On the reverse slope of Top and echeloned onto the rear, guarding the western slopes of Daruchhian was the enemy position of West Spur. An attack using the western slopes to capture Daruchhian was considered unlikely, as it involved getting behind the defender, for which an attacker would need to take a circuitous and long route. Therefore, West Spur was not initially occupied, though defensive positions had been prepared. The defensive positions would be occupied, when required, at short notice.

Pakistani troops on Top were administered with the help of mules, who would carry heavy stores to Top from the roadhead located at its base, north of Daruchhian. After unloading their stores the mules were stabled in a shed located on the northern slopes of Daruchhian, referred to as Mule Shed. Since it was located on the northern route to Top the Pakistanis had created a defensive position around it.

Except SW Spur, all other slopes of Daruchhian were thickly wooded providing good overhead cover. Though SW Spur had no trees its slopes were covered with shrubs and bushes.

Additional security to the enemy defences was provided through a well-laid-out system of wire obstacles, anti-personnel mines and booby traps.

Due to the enemy's extensive defensive preparations, capturing Daruchhian was a formidable task. To succeed, a well-trained attacker would need to coordinate and rehearse all aspects of the plan prior to launching an attack. Lt Col Inderjit's request for additional time was justified. However, since his request had been turned down, 14 Grenadiers had very limited time before being launched into battle.

~

Hamir addressing the men of his battalion.

14 Grenadiers was a relatively new battalion raised only a few years before the war. It consisted of four rifle companies, each with approximately 120 soldiers. The companies were named Alpha, Bravo, Charlie and Delta. Each company had a unique composition of soldiers. Alpha and Bravo Company commanded by Major S.R. Dogra and Major Harbans Chahal respectively comprised Rajput troops. Charlie Company

commanded by Major Hamir Singh consisted of Kaimkhani Muslims, while Delta Company composed of Dogra troops was commanded by Major M.H. Khan. For the capture of Daruchhian, in addition to his battalion, Lt Col Inderjit had been allotted one company of 6/11 GR.

The Attack Plan

Chahal's company would commence the attack. It would attack frontally along the eastern slopes of Daruchhian to capture OP Position. After capturing OP Position it would go for Daruchhian Top. The time designated to commence the attack (H Hour) was 23:00 hours on 13 December.

The task of Hamir's company was to establish a roadblock at area Pimple, a small hill near the village Sehra and be ready to capture West Spur, on orders, if required. Since Pimple was located at the rear of the enemy, the company would infiltrate into Pakistani territory, taking a circuitous route to reach Pimple. Therefore, Hamir's company would be the first company of 14 Grenadiers to enter Pakistani territory so that it could be at Pimple when Chahal's company began its attack.

Pimple was selected so that it would be able to prevent enemy interference during the battalion's attack on OP Position and Top. If at any stage the going got tough for the battalion, Hamir's company would attack West Spur, to relieve pressure.

A platoon consisting of approximately thirty men of Dogra's company led by Lieutenant Bhagwan Singh had been grouped with Hamir. They would lead Hamir's company for some time in enemy territory and thereafter secure the bridge over the nala south of Daruchhian on the Kotli–Hajira road.

A platoon of 6/11 GR had been tasked to occupy a position near Mule Shed. This platoon would prevent reinforcement of Daruchhian from the neighbouring Pakistani picket Three Star to its north. Similarly, a platoon of 7 Mahar was asked to deploy on its own side of the CFL in such a manner that it would be able to prevent reinforcement or interference from the Pakistani picket of Black Rock to its south.

The Battle

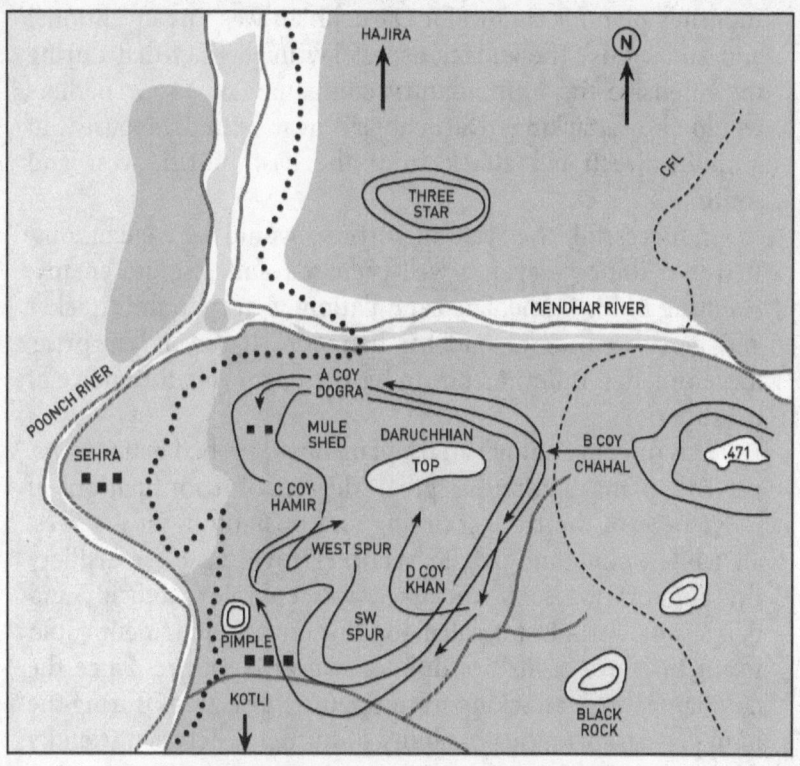

The attack plan of 14 Grenadiers. (Not to scale.)

Khan's company was tasked to capture SW Spur.

The task given to Dogra's company was to initially secure the forming-up place (FUP) of the battalion. Once the attacks commenced they would occupy Mule Shed as the battalion reserve. Since one of Dogra's platoons had been allotted to Hamir, only two platoons would be available to Dogra for his task.

Inderjit with his command group would be located in the defended area of 6/11 GR and he would control the battle from Point 471. A company of 6/11 GR was tasked as reserve to 14 Grenadiers.

Inderjit's plan for capture of Daruchhian was unconventional and audacious. The audaciousness lay in the fact that during the offensive the four infantry companies of 14 Grenadiers would be attacking Daruchhian near simultaneously in a multi-directional attack from the east, north, west and south.

If successful, the scale of surprise would be tremendous. It would unnerve even a well-prepared and resolute enemy, resulting in his immediate capitulation, victory to the attacker and glory to Inderjit and his battalion. It was no surprise, therefore, that Inderjit stuck to his plan, ignoring the advice of his superiors.

This unconventional attack plan, however, had major flaws.

The plan required a great degree of coordination of movement of the troops, timing and positioning of reserves, all while maintaining radio silence. Providing close artillery fire support for such an attack was complex, difficult and dangerous. A slight miscalculation or error of judgment could result in heavy casualties due to own artillery fire. Since the companies were attacking from opposite directions during the hours of darkness the possibility of fratricide between friendly forces could not be ruled out.

The reserve was inadequate and its location unsound. If any company failed in its task, Dogra's company, the company earmarked as reserve from within the battalion, with only two platoons, was inadequate and their location at Mule Shed was too far away. It would be unable to reach the needy company when it mattered. Therefore, if things didn't go as planned, Inderjit would have no option but to employ the company of 6/11 GR. In the short time available prior to the attack it was not possible for 14 Grenadiers to develop the rapport required in battle with the company of 6/11 GR.

Tasking Chahal's company to capture the most important tactical objective of Daruchhian Top by the most obvious frontal assault through the enemy minefield and not assigning and positioning an immediate reserve in its vicinity was a blunder.

It is an unwritten and universal law in the infantry that during an attack operation the commanding officer and his command group moves and positions itself with the major component of the assaulting troops. This reassures the troops and enables the commanding officer to exercise effective control over the battle, take corrective action on the spot, and if necessary, provide inspiration by his courage and personal leadership by leading from the front. The current plan had no such provision and the location of the commanding officer's command group at Point 471, far removed from the action, was inappropriate.

It was precisely for these reasons that the GOC, Maj Gen Kundan Singh had not been impressed with Inderjit's plan. However, Inderjit believed that his battalion was well trained and prepared for the task. He was optimistic of his battalion's success.

Orders were passed as per the plan and the battalion began its final preparations for the attack. The attack would commence with Hamir infiltrating into enemy territory with his company. Inderjit had come to respect Hamir's physical and professional abilities. His belief in Hamir had been strengthened during a recent visit of Maj Gen O.S. Kalkat, erstwhile GOC of 5 Mountain Division, where 14 Grenadiers had served earlier. Kalkat knew Hamir well and had observed his physical prowess, tactical acumen and practical knowledge while deployed at the North-East Frontier Agency (NEFA— now Arunachal Pradesh). On finding Hamir in the battalion he had made much of his abilities, praising him profusely in the presence of Inderjit. Taking cue, Inderjit had given Hamir the most physically demanding task in his attack plan.

~

Hamir was born on 27 September 1938 in a Rajput Mertia Rathore family of warriors, considered direct descendants of Rao Veeram Dev of Merta (a small principality of Rajasthan), Jaimal, Patta (of Battle of Chittaur[13] fame) and the divine princess-saint Mirabai.

A third-generation army officer, he was only a child when his father, Captain (later Major General) Kalyan Singh of 2 Field Regiment, was captured while fighting the Battle of Bir Hakeim (North Africa) in May 1942. On being captured Kalyan Singh was incarcerated in the POW camp at Aversa, Italy.

Once it became known that Kalyan Singh had been taken prisoner, the British government sent Mr A.P. Cox, principal of Chopasni School, Jodhpur to check on the well-being of his family. During his visit to Kalyan's village Mr Cox found that there were schoolgoing children in the family. He asked for them to be sent to Chopasni immediately for their education. Hamir was one of them. After his initial years at Chopasni, Hamir studied at Sadul Public School, Bikaner and Birla College, Pilani.

Though slightly built as a young child, by the time he turned eighteen he had transformed into a strapping young man, almost six feet tall. An excellent sportsman with extraordinary stamina, Hamir excelled at athletics, football and swimming. Long hours in the swimming pool and playing football had toned his muscles to perfection. When he joined the Indian Military Academy, Hamir was the clichéd tall, dark and handsome young man. In December '62 he was commissioned to 2 Grenadiers.

Due to the 1962 Sino-Indian War his father, then Brigadier Kalyan Singh, was unable to attend Hamir's Passing Out Parade at the Indian Military Academy. Instead, he wrote him a congratulatory letter. During the Sino-Indian War, Kalyan Singh had experienced loss, witnessed valour and seen the disgraceful sight of some men fleeing from battle. Therefore, in his letter to Hamir he stated his expectations unambiguously. '*Son, I can bear your loss, but not disgrace!*' he wrote and these words remained ingrained in him ever since.

His wedding was solemnized immediately after his commissioning on 1 July 1963, a common practice in those days. Strikingly beautiful and an easy conversationalist, his wife Laxmi was the eldest daughter of a police officer, Shri Jodh Singh. Her paternal grandfather, Colonel Balu Singh was the commanding officer of the Ganga Risala (later 13 Grenadiers) and aide-de-camp to the Maharaja of Bikaner, while her maternal grandfather served in the Poona Horse.

Laxmi, Hamir Singh's wife.

Hamir spent the initial two years of his service with his battalion 2 Grenadiers at Ladakh. A few months after the birth of his elder son Vikram he was ordered to report to Nasirabad to form part of a new battalion—14 Grenadiers. Accordingly, he joined the battalion on 1 January 1965.

In August 1965, 14 Grenadiers moved to NEFA, coincidentally the very same location where Hamir's father had fought the Chinese in the 1962 war. Deployed in a remote area, Hamir was unable to reach home in time for the birth of his younger son Vijay in November 1965.

During his tenure at NEFA, Hamir was selected for deputation as a Weapon Training Instructor for the Nigerian Defence Academy (NDA). He left for Kaduna, Nigeria with his young family in April 1969. After spending over two professionally satisfying and enjoyable years in Nigeria, in November 1971, Hamir and his family were in Bharatpur, India, to attend the wedding of Laxmi's younger brother.

Laxmi's father had organized a grand celebration. Kishore, the handsome bridegroom, sat majestically on a massive elephant as the baraat arrived at the wedding venue to the beating of drums and the sound of the shehnai.

'Look, mama, what a huge elephant,' Vijay shouted excitedly. His sing-song voice and British accent had already become a source of amusement to the local children.

As a toddler, Vijay had spoken his first words in Nigeria, at three years old. His young British teacher took pride in the way his vocabulary had grown in just a couple of months. Now, at Bharatpur, just shy of six years, Vijay's vocabulary was useless. The language to communicate was Hindi and Vijay didn't know a word of it. His elder sibling, however, managed his way around with a smattering of his mother tongue.

Young Vijay in Kaduna, Nigeria.

The challenge of communication though didn't prevent the boys from having a whale of a time during the wedding celebrations, while Laxmi, being the eldest in the family, was engrossed in her sisterly duties. Hamir revelled in the attention as the 'foreign-returned' son-in-law. The weather was pleasant and the large family gathering was filled with joy and happiness.

A few days after the wedding Hamir received a message from his father, Maj Gen Kalyan Singh, which left him confused. The message conveyed to him that his battalion required him to rejoin immediately. Since he was still on deputation with the NDA, he should, he reasoned, be taking his orders from the NDA. So he sought his father's advice. Maj Gen Kalyan Singh had only recently retired as the Military Secretary (MS) of the Indian Army. A veteran of many wars, he was more than qualified to counsel his son on such matters.

'Papa, I want to join my battalion. But technically I am still with Nigerian Defence Academy. Will there be any complications if I rejoin my battalion immediately?'

'No, I don't think so,' his father replied.

'Some of my colleagues aren't joining until allowed by the Nigerian government.'

'It doesn't matter what others are doing, son. You go ahead and join immediately. It's the right thing to do. Your battalion wouldn't call you if it wasn't urgent! You will never be able to forgive yourself if you don't join your battalion in a time of need. I will handle the formalities, don't worry.'

It was just the answer he needed. On the tenth of November, Hamir bid farewell to his family.

Laxmi had seen her husband leave for service in field areas many times; it was not unusual. Since their wedding she had spent most of her time alone while Hamir was stationed at Ladakh and NEFA. To her, his departure seemed normal, except that his leave had been cut short.

Goodbyes were still always sad and painful. On this occasion, perhaps even more. Having spent the last two years at Nigeria with her husband she had got used to having him around. She would miss him dearly.

13 December 1971. Point 471

On the morning of 13 December Hamir received a message that Inderjit would personally see Hamir's company off at the battalion assembly area near Point 471 that evening. The silent infiltration of Hamir's company into enemy territory was the first and most important part of the operation and Inderjit wanted to wish them luck before they left.

At 17:30 hours Inderjit addressed Hamir's company—

'Charlie Company, the task I know is tough. But then you are my best trained company and Hamir, your Company Commander, my toughest officer. I am certain there is no one more suitable for the task. Success will be yours.'

Lt Col Inderjit Singh's words seemed sincere enough. His attack plan was about to be set in motion. Speaking to Charlie Company seemed more an attempt to calm his own nerves than boosting the morale of the company itself. He needed self-assurance as his plan was risky.

'Hamir, you may proceed to your start point as scheduled. But once you reach there, wait for the final go-ahead. All the best and Godspeed.'

Hamir saluted smartly and shook hands with Inderjit. All that was left to do was to move the company to its start point and wait for Inderjit's go-ahead.

Charlie Company comprised 120 soldiers who were divided into a Company HQ and three platoons.

The Company HQ consisted of Hamir, the company commander, Subedar Taj Mohammad, who was the senior JCO, Subedar Ram Singh, the mortar fire controller (MFC), and about twenty-five other men.

The three platoons were 7, 8 and 9 Platoons led by Naib Subedar Hasim, Lieutenant Om Prakash Dalal and Naib Subedar Alam Ali. Each platoon consisted of thirty men.

Captain Jagdish Chander Gosain of 196 Mountain Regiment was the artillery FOO accompanying the company. He would control and direct the fire of artillery guns supporting Hamir's company during the attack.

The move ahead of the start point was planned late in the evening to take advantage of the fading light in concealing their movement. The first part of the move would be through own minefields, which was expected to take not more than twenty to thirty minutes. After crossing the minefields the company would spend a few minutes to regain command and control before they proceeded ahead.

'Sahab, start ka code word mil gaya hai,' Ibrahim, his radio operator, informed Hamir. *Sir, the code word to commence our move has been received.*

Hamir, who had been resting near the start point, stood up. His standing up was the indication for the rest of the company that the move would commence in a few minutes. The men stood up silently, picked up their loads, cocked their weapons and waited for Hamir's signal to start.

At exactly 18:30 hours Hamir raised his left hand up indicating that the move was commencing.

Well begun is half done. For Hamir's company well begun meant passing through own minefields successfully. A delicate task, as even one misplaced step could cause an explosion. This could be catastrophic as it would alert the enemy. Besides, a mine casualty right at the very commencement of operations wouldn't augur well for the company or the battalion.

The mines had been laid by 7 Mahar, the battalion occupying defences at Point 471. Hence, 7 Mahar was responsible for guiding 14 Grenadiers through their minefield. A guide familiar with the layout of the minefield had been arranged to assist 14 Grenadiers negotiate the minefield.

It had been arranged that Havildar Goverdhan of 14 Grenadiers would meet up with the guide of 7 Mahar. He had moved ahead earlier in the day and now stood waiting for Hamir's company to arrive. As soon as the company linked up with Goverdhan the guide commenced moving.

Despite being well acquainted with the minefield the weight of responsibility seemed to have got the better of the 7 Mahar's guide. He was understandably nervous and tentative due to which movement was slow and Hamir's company took more time than expected in negotiating the minefield.

The entire battalion was to follow the same route and stood lined up behind Hamir's company. The slow movement and delay was making the rest of the battalion restless.

Angry messages were exchanged to and fro, as the rear companies wanted Hamir's company to get a move on. Hamir was helpless as his company's move depended upon the speed of the 7 Mahar's guide.

It was nearly 20:00 hours when the company finally exited the minefield. Now they would commence their infiltration.

Troops tasked to infiltrate are required to carry the entire company's battle loads through long distances—silently. This is an unenviable task given the heavy weight and odd-shaped loads required to be carried on their backs, over and above their personal weapons and kit. This makes infiltrating troops especially vulnerable until they reach their designated hides near their objective. In the hide the non-essential loads are left behind before the actual attack.

Therefore, specially earmarked personnel are designated to protect and navigate for the infiltrating body of troops. Bhagwan's platoon would be undertaking this task for Hamir. The platoon would move about ten minutes ahead. Hamir's company would follow, secure in the knowledge that navigation and protection from the front was being taken care of by Bhagwan's platoon.

Accordingly Bhagwan's platoon had commenced infiltration immediately after crossing the minefield, while Hamir's company waited, allowing them a ten-minute lead.

Lieutenant Dalal's platoon was tasked to lead Hamir's company. The Company HQ consisting of Hamir and some essential personnel would follow immediately behind.

The move commenced at 20:10 hours and the 120 men of Charlie Company were on their way, moving stealthily and skilfully through the dense forest.

It was a dark night. The thick forests and the heavy undergrowth was making movement difficult. After forty-five minutes the column came to a halt and a messenger from Dalal's platoon reported to Hamir.

'Sir, we are not able to follow Lieutenant Bhagwan's platoon. We just can't see them,' he whispered.

This was not good. They were supposed to be in visual contact. Since radio silence was being maintained there was no scope of contacting Bhagwan through the radio.

Hamir weighed his options. He could either halt the company and send out a small team to find Bhagwan's platoon or his company would need to continue on its own. It would be too risky to send out a patrol searching for Bhagwan's platoon in enemy territory. Besides, trying to locate the platoon would be time-consuming. Their movement had been slow to begin with and there was no time to lose. Hamir had made his decision.

'Tell Lieutenant Dalal to commence the move. He will now be responsible for both security of our column as well as navigation.' Hamir was always decisive. It was one of the traits his men admired most.

'Right, sir.' The messenger disappeared into the darkness to join his platoon.

In a few moments the move re-commenced. Without the benefit of the security that Bhagwan's platoon provided, their movement slowed down further. At about 21:45 hours Hamir received a message from Inderjit.

'OC to Charlie. Speed up. Chahal is already nearing his RV.'

Chahal's company was approaching their RV—rendezvous—in accordance with the start time for the attack, which was 23:00 hours, the H Hour.

At about the same time an innocuous message was heard on the radio. 'Dilli door nahin.' *Delhi is not far.* This was a pre-arranged coded message indicating that Chahal's company had arrived at its RV. They had reached before time.

It had been planned that by the time Chahal commenced his attack, Hamir's men would be deployed in area Pimple, behind Daruchhian. Hamir's company would support Chahal in two ways. Initially, as Chahal attacked, they would prevent any move of Pakistani reinforcements towards Daruchhian.

Secondly, should Chahal find the going difficult, Hamir's company could be launched from the rear of Daruchhian to relieve pressure on his company.

Inderjit was therefore closely monitoring the progress of both companies. The transmission of the pre-arranged message meant that Chahal had rolled down Point 471 faster than expected, whereas Hamir, due to the delay at the minefield, was behind schedule.

Hamir realized that he needed to speed up the move. He made an instant decision: he would personally lead his company.

'Taj Mohammad sahab, I am going to lead now. Bring up the rear as soon as possible,' Hamir said, as he moved right at the head of the company.

'Roger, sir. I will ensure that the rest of the company is close behind,' Taj Mohammad acknowledged.

Taj Mohammad was not surprised. He was well versed with Hamir's style of leadership. Whenever required, his company commander would always lead by example.

Hamir now took over the responsibility of navigation and led his company confidently through the forests as they walked towards their RV—Pimple, code-named 'Kala Chor'.

~

Harbans Chahal was pleased with the way his company had started out. They had followed Hamir's company in accordance with the schedule of the move. His men, all charged up and confident, had climbed down Point 471 faster than expected. Neck had been secured smoothly, without an incident. The operation had so far proceeded with clockwork precision, as a result of which they now had about ten minutes to spare. They lay dispersed close to the FUP, waiting for the H Hour which was scheduled at 23:00 hours. Since they were in enemy territory and close to their defences it was imperative that their presence remain concealed. Messages were conveyed by touch and torches were forbidden.

The entire battalion was now waiting to hear the code word

'Kala Chor' from Hamir's company, which would indicate that they had reached their RV. The code word was expected any moment as the H Hour was just ten minutes away. Inderjit finally lost his patience and called out—'OC to Charlie, report your location.'

'Charlie to OC, we are still approximately a kilometre from "Kala Chor",' Hamir replied, calmly.

'Roger, Roger. Reach "Kala Chor" quickly. Bravo will now start for Delhi thirty-five minutes later than scheduled,' Inderjit declared. His message meant that the H Hour for the attack was now 23:35 hours. He needed to confirm whether Chahal had registered the change in the H Hour. He called out to him. 'OC for Bravo, confirm you have understood the fresh H Hour.'

'Yes, Bravo, confirmed. Over,' Chahal replied, looking at his wrist watch. There were still forty-five minutes left.

As he settled down to rest he smiled to himself. It was surprising how his destiny was linked with Hamir once again. His mind wandered back to February 1956 when Hamir and he had been students together at Birla College, Pilani.

February 1956. Birla College Stadium, Pilani

'Last call for the 100 Final. All participants are requested to report to their lanes immediately.'

The announcement could hardly be heard amidst the loud cheering as the 100-metre final was about to start. The reigning champion Ranbir Singh of Birla Arts College confidently took his place on lane number 3, while Hamir, representing Birla Science College, lined up in lane number 4. As soon as all participants had settled into their respective lanes the starter pistol was fired. To the surprise of the spectators Hamir led right from the beginning, easily winning the sprint with a lead of over a yard. Now the Science College supporters had found their voice and the stadium reverberated with cheers for Hamir.

Ranbir, the reigning champion had lost, angering the

Arts College coach. The unexpected loss had allowed the Science College to claw back into the reckoning for the overall championship, joining the Arts College at the top of the leaderboard.

The championship would now be decided by the discus throw final, which was the penultimate event. The main competition was expected to be between Hamir Singh of Science College and Harbans Chahal of Arts College.

Hamir was naturally athletic and had been fortunate in receiving his early education at Chopasni. A visionary school of its time, Chopasni had an excellent sports culture and the easy access to coaching at Chopasni helped Hamir further hone his sporting skills.

Harbans Chahal on the other hand had had a late introduction to organized sports. A simple, likeable young lad, Chahal belonged to a farming family based in Mohanpura, near Sri Ganganagar, Rajasthan. On joining the Arts College his tall six-foot-two frame immediately drew the attention of the sports coach. In a short while Harbans became an active member of the athletics team representing the college in the javelin, discus throw and shot put events. What he lacked in technique he more than made up for through sheer hard work and commitment. His main competitor, more often than not, was Hamir. Whenever Chahal lost to Hamir his coach would taunt him endlessly.

Having lost the 100-metre event the Arts College coach was already frustrated and angry. To make matters worse Chahal was having a bad day and his throws were subpar. It was now time for his final throw.

'C'mon Chahal! Puri jaan laga ke phenk,' the coach yelled. *Throw it with all your strength.* He wasn't done yet. As Chahal entered the arena the coach remarked loud enough for the spectators to hear—'Sports diet kha kha kar saandh ban gaya hai. Dum hai toh dikha. Bahut ho gaya.' *Do something, if you have it in you. Enough of this. You have just become an overfed bull gorging on the sports diet.*

The coach's words seemed to have had the desired effect.

Chahal flung the discus with a vengeance. It spun vigorously as it cut through the air and landed well ahead of all flag markers. He had broken the college record! As the officials raised the green flag indicating a fair throw the spectators rose to give Chahal a thunderous applause. His coach ran up to him and hugged him joyously.

Hamir, the final competitor of the day, walked up for his final throw. He gripped the discus in his hand and limbered up for a while. When he was ready he bent low, rotated around his axis and smoothly released the discus at a slightly higher angle than his previous throws. There was a hush among the spectators as the discus reached the highest point in its trajectory. By the time it began descending it was clear that it was a good throw. It landed just ahead of the flag marking Chahal's best effort. His record had been broken and so was Harbans Chahal, who collapsed on the ground in despair.

Hamir walked out the arena quietly, he had always been a shy winner. While he enjoyed each victory his emotions were rarely obvious. As the spectators cheered, Hamir observed some of his college mates walk up towards Chahal, who was distraught. One among them decided to vent his anger on Chahal.

'Oye Chahal, rahne de yeh athletics-shetletics. Tu wapas apne khet ja aur hal chala! Yo tere bas ki nahin hai, bhai!' he taunted. *Forget about athletics. Just go back to your village and plough your fields. This is not your cup of tea.* The other boys accompanying him broke out into peals of laughter.

Harbans Chahal was devastated. Hamir walked up to him and sat down beside him quietly, allowing him time to get over the event. After some time, he spoke.

'Utho Harbans, chalo, bahut ho gaya, bhai.' *Enough brother, let's go.* He offered him his hand, which Chahal hesitatingly accepted. As soon as the prize distribution was over Hamir convinced Chahal to accompany him to the college cafeteria.

Chahal remained withdrawn and tentative for a while. It took a plate of samosas and delicious jalebis to break the ice between them. By the time they had finished they had become

Hamir standing on the podium as winner and Harbans Chahal (left) as runner-up after the discus throw event.

Hamir won so many prizes at the Birla College sports meet, instead of calling him for each medal, they decided to give him all of them together on a tray later.

good friends. Thereafter, along with Ranbir, they became the stars of all local sporting events, where their individual positions would depend on the performance of the others.

After college they had lost touch with each other until destiny brought them together to 14 Grenadiers.

In a strange coincidence their actions in the battlefield of Daruchhian were once again closely interlinked, as they were many years ago at Birla College, Pilani. Only this time, Hamir was lagging behind Chahal.

Speed up, Hamir ji, we have got to win this too, Chahal said to himself, as he waited for his college mate to reach his RV.

~

Even though the H Hour of Chahal's Company had been delayed to 23:35 hours, Hamir, who was leading his company, realized that he would need to increase the pace. He began walking faster. The men at the rear of the column were finding it difficult to keep up, breaking into a slow jog from time to time.

They had just covered 500 yards or so when Hamir tripped on a wire. Expecting it to be a booby trap, everyone dived for cover, waiting for an explosion. Surprisingly, nothing happened.

On close examination they realized that the wire was in fact a telephone cable. Its alignment suggested that it provided telephone connectivity between Daruchhian and the neighbouring Pakistani picket of Black Rock. A beaten track existed along the telephone cable and fresh footmarks indicated that it was being checked on frequently.

Since telephone cables are normally laid along the shortest distance, following the cable could have been the quickest way to Daruchhian Top. It was a tempting option but Hamir decided against it. Being the most obvious route to Top it could well lead to a trap laid by the enemy. He would continue with the more circuitous route, as planned. After quickly snipping off the telephone cable the company continued its march forward.

They were now moving along the nala south of Daruchhian. Navigation was easier and progress was good. The route they had chosen required getting across the nala just prior to their arrival at Pimple. In a short while they were at the crossing site and Pimple was just another 500 yards away.

Crossing the nala in darkness with their heavy loads required considerable skill and effort. The banks of the nala were reasonably steep and silence was of paramount importance as they were close to the enemy defences.

The leading platoon with Hamir had now reached area Three Huts at the outskirts of Sehra village, from where area Pimple was visible. Since the nala was an obstacle, before they continued ahead they were required to check whether everyone had crossed over. Hamir called out to Dalal and said, 'Dalal please take stock of the company while I prepare for the onward move.'

'Roger, sir,' Dalal replied. When Dalal did a headcount he realized that a part of the company had been left behind. He turned back, retracing his steps to the nala to speed up the crossing. He looked at his watch. They had just fifteen minutes before Chahal's H Hour—23:35 hours.

~

Chahal was still lost in the thoughts of his days at Birla College when his radio operator nudged him, 'Sahab, it's 23:15 hours. We need to proceed to the FUP.'

Chahal stood up and began walking towards the FUP. The entire company followed and silently began forming up astride him. It was a cold winter night and Chahal's stomach was tied in knots as he watched his men form up for the attack. His nervousness was understandable. His company was leading the battalion's attack. How his attack went would have a major impact on the battalion's performance.

Exactly at 23:35 hours the artillery guns supporting Chahal's attack began firing. The valley suddenly came alive to the loud sounds of explosions echoing in the distance. The attack on OP Position had begun. The men moved silently, like ghosts in the night. The occasional rustling of the leaves or snapping of the twigs was the only giveaway that a large body of troops was on the move. The slope was steep and the dew had made it slippery. Movement had to be deliberate and they paused from time to time ensuring that they were together.

They had successfully reached within 100 yards of OP Position. *So far so good*, Chahal thought, *if our luck lasts for a few more minutes we will be at our objective*. As they climbed further they found themselves at the base of a steep cliff. Chahal signalled his company to halt while he planned his next move.

He turned back looking for his operator who had been trailing behind. Seeing his company commander waiting the operator hurried towards him, losing his balance in the process. He fell heavily and seemed hurt. Chahal rushed to help. As soon as he took his first step there was a loud explosion, knocking Chahal to the ground. He had stepped on a mine.

The soldiers rushed to their company commander, who lay writhing in unbearable pain. His foot was badly disfigured and there was heavy bleeding.

Meanwhile, on hearing the sound of the explosion the enemy at Top and OP Position realized that they were being attacked from the direction of Neck. They opened up with all their weapons on a hapless Bravo Company. The enemy had meticulously covered the approach to OP Position with automatic weapons. Their automatic fire played havoc on the attackers, as did the Pakistani artillery guns, which opened up too. The fire was effective and deadly. Chahal's company suffered heavy casualties.

Amidst the fire, a couple of men lifted their company commander and placed him in a broken enemy bunker they found nearby. He was given some water to drink while a soldier from the medical section tended to his wounds. As Chahal lay injured in the disused enemy bunker, fifty yards short of OP Position, his radio operator called out to Inderjit—'Bravo for OC. Over.'

'OC for Bravo, pass your message. Over!' an excited Inderjit replied. He had been optimistically waiting for news of their success.

'Bravo, Chahal sahab mine se ghayal ho gaye hain. Unka pair buri tarah se damage ho gaya hai. Over.' *Major Chahal has been wounded by a mine. His foot is badly mangled.*

A serious injury to the company commander right at the beginning of the attack was disastrous. Surprise had been lost and the enemy alerted to the attack. The Indians had dared to attack the Pakistani post from the most obvious direction and the Pakistanis were more than ready. They let Chahal's company have it.

~

Hamir waited at area Three Huts as the remaining platoons started arriving in penny packets. Dalal was still at the crossing site, hustling the company across the nala.

The rear of the company was being brought up by Subedar Taj Mohammad. His crossing over would indicate that the entire company was in. Dalal strained his eyes in the darkness eagerly looking for him. Taj Mohammad had just about reached the crossing site when artillery fire opened up in the distance. It was 23:35 hours and Chahal's attack had commenced. A worried Hamir contacted Dalal on the radio, 'Dalal, please ask the rear to speed up. The attack has commenced. We need to deploy as soon as possible.'

Before Dalal could reply, artillery shells began bursting around them.

'Disperse! Take cover!' Hamir yelled.

The ground shook violently as each high-explosive-filled projectile detonated, sending hundreds of splinters in all directions.

Hamir was perplexed. *How had the Pakistanis discovered our company?* He had taken great pains to ensure stealth while moving into enemy territory. Now that his company had been located, an enemy ground attack was inevitable. The situation was deeply concerning and Hamir hurriedly deployed the men where they were.

The men lay dispersed, nervously scanning the area. They had no idea which direction the enemy would choose for the attack. They waited anxiously with their fingers on their triggers.

It had been over fifteen minutes since the artillery fire. There were no signs of a ground attack. Something wasn't quite right. Captain Gosain, who had been observing the manner in which the explosions were taking place seemed to have figured out the reason. He moved up to Hamir and whispered, 'Sir, you know what? The artillery fire we were subjected to was from our own guns!'

'C'mon Gosain, how could that be possible?' Hamir retorted.

'I am absolutely certain, sir. You see, we are now directly behind Daruchhian, which is being engaged by our guns to assist the attack on OP Position. Though their target is Daruchhian Top, the shells which overshoot the target are falling on us!'

Hamir realized what Gosain was saying seemed logical. The shells falling on them had been exploding a few seconds after the ones at Top. There was a definite link. It also explained the absence of a ground attack.

'Well, at least our infiltration hasn't been detected,' Hamir remarked.

The firing stopped after a while. This was the respite Hamir was looking for. He gave orders to resume their advance towards the RV. They had moved some distance when Ibrahim asked Hamir to stop. 'Sir, there's no one following us. Lieutenant Dalal hasn't returned as yet,' he remarked.

Hamir turned around to look. Except for Ibrahim, Captain Gosain and his operator, there was no one following. Apparently, due to the artillery shelling the men who were in the process of crossing the nala got stuck at the crossing site.

'Sir, I will fetch them,' Gosain volunteered.

'Thank you, Gosain. Please get them as soon as possible.'

Gosain headed back to the nala where he found Dalal busy gathering the men. Taj Mohammad was in, indicating that the entire company had successfully negotiated the nala. Miraculously the company had escaped unhurt from their first encounter with live fire. Having reached the RV the company crossed the Kotli–Hajira road and by 00:15 hours they were in the process of deploying at Pimple, from where they would undertake their tasks.

At this stage Chahal's company was already in the thick of battle at OP Position.

~

With Chahal seriously wounded short of OP Position, Bravo Company was in a precarious situation. Messages were exchanged on the radio between Chahal's company and the Battalion HQ. Inderjit wanted the company to make a last push to capture OP Position. However, the heavy casualties and relentless enemy fire was making it impossible.

'C'mon Bravo, keep advancing,' Inderjit pleaded.

'Sir, we have come under heavy fire. There's heavy automatic fire from the stone bunker on Top. We have had many casualties,' Chahal's radio operator replied. In the absence of his company commander the radio operator was the only one in communication with Inderjit and he sounded desperate.

'Don't worry. Maintain contact with the enemy. I am sending another company to help you,' Inderjit replied, trying to reassure him.

'Roger, please hurry, we have very few men left,' the radio operator pleaded.

'What's your exact location, Bravo?' Inderjit inquired.

'We are in a disused enemy bunker about fifty yards from the enemy LMG post at OP Position. Major Chahal is with me. He's bleeding profusely. He needs immediate help,' the radio operator said.

'Roger, I am working on it.'

Hamir, who had been listening to the radio exchange, was saddened to hear about Chahal's injury. *Chahal is a tough man, I am sure he will come through*, he hoped.

Inderjit assessed the situation. It was now 00:30 hours. The frontal attack of Chahal's company had been stalled short of OP Position. Hamir's company should have reached its location by now. Major Dogra's company was on the move towards Mule Shed. *That's it!* It struck him. *If I can get Dogra to move his company towards Neck, instead of Mule Shed, I will be able to ease the pressure on Chahal's company.*

'Dogra sahab ko contact karo!' Inderjit ordered his radio operator. *Call Dogra Sahab.*

'OC for Alpha. Over,' the operator called out. There was no reply. He tried again but there was no reply whatsoever. He kept trying, without luck.

~

Dogra's company, after having secured the FUP for Chahal's company, was on the move to Mule Shed. They were required to remain deployed at Mule Shed as a reserve for the battalion.

Since they were traversing through a valley they were temporarily out of communication with the Battalion HQ.

Due to the battle taking place between Chahal's company and the enemy at OP Position, all the enemy posts were on the alert. To ward off an attack the enemy posts resorted to random speculative fire with their automatic weapons.

The company's move along the valley had not been detected. It was now time for them to climb up the slope towards Mule Shed. They climbed cautiously and were now within 200 yards of Mule Shed when an enemy MMG carrying out speculative fire shot a burst in the direction of Dogra. He was hit on his chest and fell critically injured.

Dogra's company returned fire, triggering an intense firefight with the enemy at Mule Shed. The enemy was now certain that they were under an attack and opened up with their artillery as well.

Dogra's senior JCO, Bhanwar Singh managed to crawl up to Dogra amidst all the firing. It was imperative to take him to a safe place, where he could be treated. He was in the process of lifting an almost lifeless Major Dogra when an artillery shell burst near them. Dogra was killed instantaneously and Bhanwar Singh seriously injured. Almost simultaneously, Dogra's radio operator attempting to close in with Bhanwar Singh stepped on a minefield and was wounded too.

The only other officer in the company, Lieutenant Ravi Tushir, was bringing up the rear. Although he had heard the firing, he was oblivious to the disaster that had struck his company. He continued moving towards Mule Shed until he stepped on a mine and had to be evacuated.

In a matter of minutes all key personnel of Dogra's company had been killed or grievously wounded. The company was in disarray. The sole reserve Inderjit had kept from within his battalion had become non-operational. The only option left to help Chahal was to immediately launch Hamir's company from the rear.

'Hamir, commence attack on West Spur, immediately,' he ordered.

'Wilco, we are moving now,' Hamir replied.

Hamir, like the rest of the battalion, had no idea what had happened to Dogra's company, which was supposed to be the battalion reserve; hence he was a bit surprised with Inderjit's decision to launch him for the attack earlier than expected. It was not even 01:00 hours.

Meanwhile, hearing Hamir's voice on the radio stirred a fading Chahal.

'Hamir ji, jaldi aao, bhai. Mujhe mere dost ki jaroorat hai!' he pleaded. *Hamir, come fast, brother. I need you, my friend!*

'Aa raha hoon, Harbans, abhi aaya!' Hamir replied. *I am coming, Harbans, just coming!*

'Please come fast, bhai, only you can help me,' Chahal pleaded. He then began rambling about their college days. Hamir realized that Chahal was delirious and close to his end. It was heart-wrenching.

'*I am on my way, Harbans. I will be there I promise. Just hang on, pal.*'

Hamir felt miserable and helpless. There was no way of reaching Chahal quickly. It was one of the major flaws of the attack plan. All he could do was keep Chahal's hopes alive.

Hamir gave out his confirmatory orders and soon Charlie Company set out for the base of West Spur from where they would head for Top.

Meanwhile, back in Alwar, Hamir's elder son Vikram was having a nightmare.

Alwar, India

'Mama, mama!'

Vikram's frightened voice woke Laxmi up. He seemed terrified. It was past midnight and he was obviously having a nightmare. Laxmi placed her hand on his forehead, gently waking him up.

Laxmi had gone through a tough evening as Vikram had accidentally got his ankle stuck between the pedal and the chain of his bicycle. Bleeding profusely, he was rushed to the hospital. The wound required a stitch or two. But even getting hold of Vikram for the mandatory tetanus injection was a challenge in itself. A timely bribe of an ice cream ensured cooperation for the necessary medical attention.

Later that evening, due to his discomfort Vikram had trouble sleeping. So when he got up screaming Laxmi assumed his ankle was the cause.

'What happened, beta? Does your ankle still hurt?' Laxmi queried.

'No mama, it's papa.'

'Papa?' Laxmi was a bit taken aback.

'Haan, mama! Two soldiers are holding him down,' he said, sobbing. 'He's trying hard to come back to us but he can't!'

'Don't worry, son. He's in his unit and fine. You just had a nightmare. Come here.' Laxmi pulled him close and kissed him on his forehead. She patted his back, gently humming him to sleep.

Taking care of two hyperactive children alone was quite a challenge for Laxmi and it took up most of her time. Although it had been almost a month since Hamir's departure, she hadn't had the time to miss him. It suddenly struck her that she had not received a single letter from him. That was definitely a bit unusual.

Vikram's nightmare had sent a shiver down her spine. As she lay down in between her children in the early hours of the fourteenth of December, she worried about her husband and missed him dearly.

Saabji, I love you. May God be with you, always, she prayed.

~

By 01:15 hours Hamir's company had formed up at the base of West Spur, ready to commence its attack.

From where the company was deployed, Top, the apex of Daruchhian, was more than 1,000 yards away. To reach Top they would need to first capture West Spur, which was expected to be occupied by the Pakistanis. Hamir's first objective, therefore, was West Spur. Once it was captured they would go for Top.

Khan's company would be attacking SW Spur which was approximately 800–1,000 yards to Hamir's right.

The objectives of Hamir's company—West Spur—and that of Major Khan's company—SW Spur—merged into a relatively flat piece of ground on which a basketball court had been constructed for recreation for Pakistani soldiers. From the basketball court, Top was just a short vertical climb of about 100–150 yards.

As Hamir stood facing Top, Dogra's objective—Mule Shed—was to his left, about 800 yards away. Hamir was not aware that Dogra's attack had petered out. He assumed that Mule Shed was under the control of Dogra's company and, therefore, his left flank was secure.

Hamir deployed his company for the attack. Dalal's platoon would lead on the spine of the spur followed by Hamir and his Company HQ. Alam Ali's platoon would advance along the left of the spur while Naib Subedar Hasim's platoon would move on the right of the spur.

After ensuring that everyone was in position and ready,

Hamir waved to his men to commence their advance. They began climbing up West Spur, moving cautiously, yard by yard. Although the treeline shielded them from enemy observation they needed to be as silent as possible, as surprising the enemy would make their task much easier. To retain surprise the company had been instructed to hold fire unless fired upon by the enemy.

They had just covered a distance of about 200 yards when someone from the left flank shouted the battalion war cry: 'Sarvada Shaktishali!'

The war cry was followed by an exchange of fire. This was most unexpected as they were still about 800 yards short of the objective. *Why had Alam Ali's platoon disobeyed the orders?* Hamir wondered.

The senior JCO, Taj Mohammad, equally surprised, contacted Alam Ali to find out what was going on. Apparently, Alam Ali's platoon had encountered a Pakistani mortar position during their move. The unexpected contact had shocked both the attacker and the defender resulting in the exchange of fire. But the sudden appearance of Alam Ali's platoon had spooked the Pakistanis occupying the mortar position into abandoning it.

However, the more pressing concern for Hamir was that the brief exchange of fire was likely to have alerted the enemy. It was for the first time that the enemy would know that an attack was building up from the west of Daruchhian. And that was exactly what happened.

A barrage of enemy artillery shells began raining down on their position. The Pakistanis were using airburst ammunition, which meant that the shells would burst above the trees with their splinters showering downwards. Periodically one could hear the tinny sound of splinters making their way through the foliage. But the dense treeline prevented the splinters from injuring them and they came out unscathed yet again as they arrived near the defences of West Spur.

The unexpected direction and speed of movement of Hamir's company had surprised the enemy. As a result, although defences had been prepared for a platoon worth of men, West Spur had not been reinforced. The defence was left to just the eight to ten enemy soldiers who were holding the position.

As the leading men of Dalal's platoon closed in on the enemy's trenches they were fired upon. Only when the platoon returned fire did the Pakistanis realize that they were being attacked by a much larger force and they fled towards Top and Mule Shed. Within no time Hamir's men were right on top of the enemy trenches, successfully capturing them.

While the men were reorganizing themselves Hamir found that other than Dalal's platoon and the Company HQ, only a few other men had fetched up. Hasim's platoon was still some distance away. And there was no sign of Alam Ali's platoon after their encounter with the enemy at the mortar position.

Unable to contact Alam Ali through the radio, Hamir dispatched Taj Mohammad to locate him. The search party returned thirty minutes later with the news that Alam Ali's platoon could not be traced. They would now have to manage without them and Hamir readjusted the defensive positions accordingly.

~

Located at Point 471, Inderjit had heard the exchange of fire on West Spur. The poor run of luck of the battalion and lack of information from Hamir's company had made him sceptical and he assumed the worst. It was nearing 03:00 hours; restless, he called Hamir, eager to know what was happening.

'OC for Charlie, what's your situation? Over,' Inderjit inquired.

'Charlie, we have captured West Spur,' Hamir replied.

Inderjit couldn't believe what Hamir was saying! Excited, he called out—'Charlie, please indicate your position. Fire a flare.'

Hamir's company fired a round of his signal pistol and the sky was illuminated by a green flare which was visible immediately behind Daruchhian Top. Inderjit was delighted. Hamir was actually on West Spur, providing 14 Grenadiers its first success.

'Charlie, shabaash. Excellent,' Inderjit complimented Hamir.

'Now hold on to your position at all costs. Hold on till the last man's last round,' he ordered. 'Khan's company is on its way to SW Spur on your right. Once SW Spur is captured the two of you must capture Top.'

Inderjit sounded happy, his confidence had been restored. The capture of Daruchhian now entirely depended on the exploitation of the success that Hamir's company had achieved. He was certain that together Hamir and Khan would be able to achieve success.

Meanwhile, Harbans Chahal's voice was once again heard on the radio.

'Hamir, aa rahe ho na? Main intezar kar raha hoon,' he said. *You are coming, aren't you? I am waiting for you.*

'Datey raho, bhai. Bas ab thodi der aur,' Hamir replied. *Hang in there brother, just a little longer.*

'Thanks, Hamir, I always knew you would come for me,' Chahal replied, his voice barely audible. Hamir realized that Chahal had hardly any time left. *Farewell, brother*, he prayed silently, *may you find peace!*

Chahal passed away a few minutes later. The brave soldier lay only fifty yards short of his objective.

The death of their company commander did not prevent the soldiers of Chahal's company from making repeated attempts to capture their objective. The senior JCO of the company Sub Jai Singh and a platoon commander Second Lieutenant G.P. Bahukhandi also lost their lives in the effort.

~

Khan's company was brimming with confidence and in high spirits. They had already proved their mettle on the night of 6/7 December when they had destroyed a Pakistani supply depot at Atian, deep into enemy territory. The company had earned kudos for their performance and Major M.H. Khan was awarded a Vir Chakra for his gallantry during the raid.

The company had set out for SW Spur as scheduled at

01:15 hours. They had planned to follow the exact same route as Hamir's company, till they reached the base of SW Spur. Thereafter they would climb up the slopes of SW Spur, which is when their real challenge would begin.

Since the slopes of SW Spur lacked tree cover, any movement on these slopes could easily be spotted from Top. Therefore, to avoid detection they would need to capture SW Spur, link up with Hamir's company and then go for Daruchhian Top—all during the hours of darkness. This meant that they needed to move fast. The challenge, however, was the dense undergrowth of shrubs and bushes which severely impeded movement.

As expected, the first leg of their journey was quick. Following Hamir's trail had been easy since a beaten track had formed due to the footsteps of the many soldiers of Hamir's company who had preceded them on their way to West Spur.

By about 03:30 hours Khan found himself standing next to the telephone cable that Hamir had stumbled upon earlier in the night and the same dilemma struck him. *Should we continue on the planned route or use the footpath along the cable?*

The daunting task of climbing the shrub-infested slopes of SW Spur nudged them towards their decision—they would follow the telephone cable. The leading platoon now switched to their new route, moving on the footpath along the telephone cable, which they hoped would provide them the shortest approach to the defences of SW Spur/Top.

As they moved ahead they found themselves in front of a wooden gate which had been shut. Seeing it shut the leading troops took the opportunity to rest a while, while the rest of the company caught up. Meanwhile the soldier leading the company forced the gate open and walked a few yards ahead to enable the platoon to get back into its tactical formation.

He had walked about ten yards when there was a loud explosion—he had stepped on a mine. The soldier was severely injured and in intense pain. Khan organized his immediate evacuation, sending him back to the start point. Satisfied with the arrangements for the soldier's evacuation Khan recommenced the move and the company was on its way. They began climbing up towards their objective—SW Spur—on the most difficult leg of their journey.

As they began closing in on their objective artillery guns supporting their attack started firing on SW Spur. Some of these rounds overshot their objective and fell on Hamir's location at West Spur. Khan's company moved rapidly and was soon in proximity of the basketball ground.

~

Hamir had just about deployed his company on West Spur when artillery shells began falling on his position once again. Whether it was the artillery guns supporting Khan's company or Pakistani guns targeting them, Hamir wasn't too sure. But the outcome was equally disastrous as a large number of his soldiers were exposed.

The enemy trenches that they had captured and occupied were just about sufficient for one platoon, whereas there were almost two platoons worth of Hamir's company in the area. The casualties were causing panic in the men due to which Hamir found that some of his men began crowding around him. For some reason they felt safe in his proximity. He kept chasing them away but some would return. Just as he thought he had sent all of them away, he was shocked to find a young soldier standing next to him. He seemed dazed and stood trembling.

'What are you doing here, soldier? You need to disperse. C'mon, move!' Hamir shouted, trying to shake him out of his obvious stupor. The soldier, however, remained motionless, mumbling incoherently.

'Sahab, bacha lo, mujhe marna nahin hai!' he begged. *Sir, save me, I don't want to die!*

'Tumhe kuch nahi hoga, Jawan, tum aad pakdo!' Hamir reassured him. *Nothing will happen to you, soldier. Take cover.*

'Mujhe maa ke paas jana hai! Unka aur koi nahin hai, woh akeli nahin reh payegi. Please bacha lo, sahab!' he continued.

I want to go home to my mother. She has no one other than me. She will not be able to live without me. Please save me, sir.

'Suno, beta, yahan khade hone se hum dono marey jayenge. Chalo aad pakdo,' Hamir pleaded. *Listen, son, if we continue standing here we will both be killed. C'mon, now take cover.*

Since the soldier wasn't registering what Hamir said, he push-shoved him trying to get him behind some cover. It was of no use, he remained frozen to the spot. Hamir moved away just in time as a shell fell at the exact same place killing the poor boy instantaneously.

~

Khan was unaware that the mine explosion earlier in the night had alerted the enemy and his movement was being monitored. The Pakistanis were waiting patiently for an opportune moment to open fire.

At 04:30 hours, Khan's company emerged near the basketball ground, having traversed the steep and shrub-infested slopes of SW Spur. The basketball ground was in a relatively flat and open part of SW Spur. The moment the company stepped onto its openness the enemy artillery opened up, and Khan's men were sitting ducks. In the absence of trees the airburst ammunition proved especially deadly, causing heavy casualties.

When the artillery firing stopped Khan rallied his men in an attempt to attack the enemy bunkers. As they closed in towards the bunkers, an enemy heavy machine gun opened up. The men returned fire, but the HMG bunker was well protected rendering their firing ineffective. They would have to wait for an opportune moment to close in on the bunkers and lob a few grenades through the portholes.

After a few minutes the HMG stopped firing. This was the moment Khan was waiting for and he rushed towards the bunker. Unfortunately for him the enemy soldiers covering the HMG from a neighbouring bunker were alert. They caught Khan's movement and fired, killing him instantaneously. It was the sad end of yet another brave company commander. It was left to his radio operator to convey the sad news to Inderjit.

'Sahab, Khan sahab shaheed ho gaye hain!' he announced. *Sir, Khan sahab has been martyred.*

This time there was no response from Inderjit. The news couldn't have been worse. His plan was in tatters. Two company commanders had been killed in action and a third grievously wounded. Three of his four companies were ineffective, pinned down, leaderless and separated from each other by vast distances, ruling out the possibility of collecting and regrouping the remnants to reinforce Hamir. Inderjit himself was located too far away in the defended area of 6/11 GR to intervene.

Hamir was now the only company commander alive and in capturing West Spur his company had provided 14 Grenadiers its only success. He was Inderjit's last hope.

~

The Pakistani soldiers who had abandoned the defences of West Spur had conveyed the information that a large body of troops was on its way to Top. When Hamir indicated his position with his signal pistol, the Pakistanis realized that Hamir's company had occupied the Pakistani defences of West Spur. They knew the area like the back of their hand, and now had a fair idea about the location of Hamir's company.

Hamir's company was now the only threat to Top as the Indian threat in all other directions had been neutralized. The Pakistanis concentrated all their efforts to dislodge Hamir's company. At 05:00 hours the artillery opened up, pounding Hamir's location mercilessly.

The abandoned enemy position which they were now at offered space for only a platoon worth of men. These bunkers were largely occupied by Hasim's platoon and Company HQ personnel who were deployed squarely facing Top. Some of Lieutenant Dalal's platoon who were deployed facing Top found space in the bunkers; the rest were deployed facing Mule Shed. Alam Ali's platoon of course had yet to established contact.

Amidst the shelling, Hamir went from position to position, trying to help the men make the most of the cover available, encouraging them to hold on to their positions. The natural cover and rocky terrain, however, provided scant protection and they suffered heavy casualties. Subedar Hasim and eight other soldiers lost their lives.

At about 05:30 hours the firing ceased. They were still attending to the injured and dead when Ram Singh rushed up to Hamir and said—'Sir, there's some noise from the direction of Mule Shed.'

As per Inderjit's plan Dogra's company was to be the reserve at Mule Shed. However, Hamir was not aware that things had not gone as planned. He assumed that the movement from Mule Shed was of Dogra's company, coming to join him. Once the two companies linked up they would have the required numbers to capture Top.

'Theek hai. It must be Major Dogra's company. Dalal, please ensure link-up with them,' Hamir remarked.

The password for any link-up within 14 Grenadiers had been pre-decided. One party would say '*Ek aur Char*' (One and Four), the number of the battalion, to which the other party would reply, '*Sarvada Shaktishali*', the battle cry of the Grenadiers.

The approaching party closed in and their footsteps could be heard. They were now only about thirty yards apart and it was time for the passwords to be exchanged.

'Sarvada Shaktishali!' Dalal called out, just loud enough for the other party to hear. The incoming party froze. There was absolute silence.

He tried again. 'Ek aur Char!' Still no response.

'Sarvada Shaktishali!' he repeated, this time in a louder voice.

'Yaa Ali, yaa Ali!' was the reply, and all hell broke loose. It was not Dogra's company but an enemy patrol.

The furious exchange of fire lasted only about fifteen minutes. Dalal and his platoon fought bravely. However, Dalal was fatally wounded during the attack and died a few minutes later. The Pakistani patrol fled, surprised to have encountered a furious Indian ambush.

Hamir was saddened by Dalal's loss. He had conversed with him just moments ago and he was brimming with confidence. His sudden death was a devastating loss of an enterprising, fearless and sincere young officer. He would be especially missed by his men, to whom he was a reassuring presence.

The first enemy patrol having been beaten back, the men had just about settled in when another enemy patrol appeared, this time from the direction of Sehra village.

To Hamir's surprise this time the enemy attack was accompanied by mortar fire from the mortar position which had supposedly been captured by Alam Ali's platoon. This confused Hamir. Alam's platoon hadn't joined the company yet. Therefore fire from the mortar position meant that either Alam Ali's platoon had been overrun or they had abandoned the mortar position. Hamir asked Gosain to bring down fire on the mortar position, which he did and after a few rounds the mortar stopped firing.

However, the skirmish with the enemy continued and the enemy patrol started closing in. Hamir deployed his company in a defensive position about fifty yards in diameter. The men stood their ground and fought fiercely. The second enemy attack eventually lost steam and the patrol was pushed back. Sporadic firing, however, continued between the two sides for the next two hours.

~

At about 07:30 hours a third enemy patrol approached their position from the direction of the mortar position. Hamir's depleted company was soon fighting another tough battle for survival. Seeing the enemy close in Hamir moved out of his cover to carry out some defensive readjustments.

The moment he left cover he was struck by an LMG burst. The bullets hit him on his right arm and his weapon fell on the ground. Surprisingly Hamir felt no pain and he reached out to pick up his weapon, but his hand wouldn't obey. Puzzled, he looked at his hand. His wrist was covered in blood and the bones were shattered. Most of the flesh around the bones had disappeared, exposing the bones. It was a gory sight. He had probably damaged his radial nerve too, which explained the lack of pain. Caught in the middle of a raging battle Hamir had neither the time nor the opportunity to tend to his injuries.

The firefight had lasted about fifteen minutes when the enemy withdrew, allowing a temporary pause in the fighting. The three skirmishes with the enemy had resulted in casualties to both sides. The medical platoon personnel got into action treating the wounded.

The lull in battle gave Ram Singh and Gosain the time to attend to their company commander. Ram Singh dressed Hamir's wounds.

'How are you feeling, sir?' Ram Singh inquired.

'I am fine, Ram Singh, luckily the injury isn't painful,' Hamir replied. Ram Singh bandaged Hamir's hand and tied it in a sling for support.

'You are lucky, sir. The wound on the upper part of your arm is not very serious. Your wrist is the main concern, there's a lot of bleeding. You need medical attention,' Ram Singh remarked.

'Never mind. I am fine now. How are our boys, Ram Singh?'

'Sir, not too good I am afraid. Rukmu is also injured,' Ram Singh replied, pointing towards Grenadier Rukmuddin. Rukmu stood smiling, seemingly unaffected, despite having a bandaged left leg.

'I am fine, sir, just a minor wound. My LMG is working well.'

'Shabaash, Rukmu, bahut badiya!' *Well done, Rukmu, very well done!* Hamir complimented Rukmuddin, smiling at him.

Hamir had been absolutely surprised at Rukmu's performance. A wiry, small-built soldier with a mild personality, his transformation in battle was amazing. Amidst all the firing and shelling he stood fearlessly firing his LMG. Equally effective and courageous was his assistant, Ast Ali of the Pioneer Section. The repeated counterattacks had been pushed back largely due to their efforts. They remained calm through all the fighting. Their fearlessness made a big difference in the fighting ability and morale of his company.

I need to ensure that they get the recognition they deserve, Hamir made a mental note to himself. Meanwhile Taj Mohammad joined Hamir after having taken stock of the company.

'Yes, sahab, what's the situation like?' Hamir queried.

'Sir, we are more or less surrounded. Remnants from the first enemy patrol are about seventy-five to hundred yards in the direction of Mule Shed,' Taj Mohammad explained.

'OK. What about Sehra village?'

Subedar Taj Mohammad comprehensively summed up the situation, 'Sir, there are still some enemy soldiers from the second skirmish in contact with us from Sehra village. The enemy bunker on Top has not been neutralized despite our best efforts. We are holding a defence line approximately fifty to seventy-five yards in diameter.'

'What about the mortar position?' Hamir inquired.

'I saw some of the enemy return towards the mortar position after the third attack but I am not sure where they are now.'

'OK, you are right, we are truly surrounded!' Hamir remarked. 'How many of us remain?'

'About forty, sir. Which includes some walking wounded like Rukmu. No idea about Subedar Alam Ali and his platoon though. They haven't joined up.'

Since the last transmission on the radio conveying the sad news about Major Khan's demise there had been no activity on the battalion radio net. Suddenly, out of the blue the radio came alive again. The voice, however, did not seem familiar.

'Charlie, Charlie, Charlie. Over.'

'Charlie, OK, pass. Over,' Hamir's operator replied.

'Charlie, humne tumhe charon ore se gher liya hai. Surrender kar do nahin toh maare jaoge!' the radio operator remarked. *We have surrounded you. You better surrender or you will be killed.* It was a Pakistani operator who had apparently stumbled upon Hamir's radio frequency.

'Tumhare sapno mein bhi hum surrender nahin karenge! Bhag jao nahin to tumhari khair nahin!' Hamir's radio operator replied, angrily. *Not even in your dreams! You'd better run, if you know what's good for you!*

If not for the seriousness of their situation the juvenile exchange between Hamir's operator and his Pakistani counterpart would have been a good source of entertainment. The verbal sparring that had commenced continued throughout the battle.

~

At 08:00 hours Subedar Alam Ali made an appearance with his platoon. They had been stuck below, on the lower slopes of West Spur. In the morning when they were on their way up they encountered the enemy counterattacking from Sehra. It was only after the counterattack had been defeated that they were able to continue. Hamir was upset by their long absence. However, Alam Ali's platoon was fresh and he would put them to use at the appropriate time. He was in the process of deploying them when he heard Ram Singh calling out to him.

'Sahab, niche dekho, kuch movement ho raha hai!' Subedar Ram Singh yelled. *Sir, look below, there's some movement.* Ram Singh had been scanning the area with his binoculars. He pointed the movement to Hamir.

At the base of West Spur near area Three Huts a column of enemy soldiers could be seen moving towards them from the very same route that Hamir and his men had used a few hours earlier.

The speed, size and timing of the previous skirmishes meant that these were undertaken by the battalion responsible for defending Daruchhian. Hamir's men had held on stubbornly despite the many casualties.

The troops approaching Hamir's position were probably from one of the neighbouring or reserve battalions. In all probability they would be fresh troops who had not taken part in the battle as yet. He estimated the approaching enemy troops to be a company worth. It indicated that the enemy now meant business and were about to launch a major counterattack.

His company's situation was now turning critical, he needed help. It would be impossible to hold on to West Spur alone. The reserve Gorkha company was required to link up with his company before the attack commenced. He made repeated attempts to speak with Inderjit. But despite his best efforts, contact could not be established.

'Now what do we do, sir?' Gosain remarked, sounding exasperated.

Hamir gave him a wry smile and said, 'You remember what the CO said? Last man, last round. That's what we will do,' he replied. 'But before that, we will target the enemy column with our artillery, when they are a little closer. Please prepare your guns accordingly.'

Gosain nodded. He contacted his CO to coordinate the fire. Gosain's CO happened to be with Brigadier Hari Singh, who, it emerged, had taken over the battle from Inderjit. Hari Singh had been waiting to speak to Hamir.

Gosain rushed to Hamir and said, 'Sir, Commander 120 is on the line. He has assumed command of the battle and he would like to speak to you.' The fact that the brigade commander had assumed command meant that the situation had drifted beyond Inderjit's control. When Hamir spoke to Hari Singh he asked him to explain what had transpired in the last few hours.

'Charlie for Tiger, situation as follows. I am left with about forty men. Many wounded, including me. I am surrounded by the enemy, who have been trying to close in. We have managed to keep them at bay so far though they remain in contact with us approximately 150–200 yards away. But we are now in a critical situation. A company of the enemy is approaching our location from the base of West Spur. They are currently about a 1,000 metres away.'

'I can give orders to engage Top with our artillery. Will that help you to capture Top?' Hari Singh inquired.

'Negative, sir. We are very close to Top, if it is engaged the shells may clear the crest of Top and fall on us. However, it will help if the guns could target the approaching enemy column once they are a bit closer,' Hamir suggested.

'Roger. I have ordered your OC to build up to your location with the reserve company of 6/11 GR. You hold on to what you have captured. I will get back to you,' Hari Singh replied.

Hamir smiled. There was no way that Inderjit and the reserve company could reach them in time. They were too far away and moving in daylight in front of the enemy would be impossible, besides being foolhardy.

Meanwhile firing had stopped and West Spur became relatively quiet. The company had been in the thick of action throughout the previous night. There would be no respite as they prepared to take on the threat manifesting from the base of West Spur. Hamir sat down, resting his back against a rock. It would take some time for the enemy to come within range of the artillery.

~

It had been almost forty-five minutes since Hamir's men had first seen the enemy closing in towards Daruchhian. The enemy was now in the process of climbing up West Spur. It seemed that the counterattack would commence within the next thirty to forty minutes.

'Gosain, it's time to target them now,' Hamir suggested. 'I will inform Brigadier Hari Singh.' Gosain nodded and began passing orders to his guns.

Hari Singh had very limited options left. When Inderjit's party moved towards Mule Shed they came under heavy fire from Three Star. To make matters worse the company of 6/11 GR was not able to fetch up due to the same reasons. Hari Singh's plan to build up Inderjit and the company of 6/11 GR in support of Hamir had to be aborted. He formulated a fresh plan and shared it with Hamir.

'I will order an air attack on Daruchhian. Immediately after the air attack you need to rush the enemy before he has time to recover. I will ask the artillery to fire some smoke rounds to cover your move.'

'Roger,' Hamir acknowledged.

It was a terrible plan. Hamir's men were hardly any distance from Top. The aerial bombardment would be as dangerous to Hamir's company as it would be to the enemy. They had already suffered many casualties due to friendly artillery fire.

Captain Gosain and Subedar Taj Mohammad, who had heard Hari Singh, were not convinced either.

'Sir, an air attack is unlikely to silence the bunkers, which are the main impediments. It's broad daylight; there is no cover between our position and Top. We will be sitting ducks!' Gosain pointed out.

'As it is we have hardly forty men left. Besides, our ammunition will be over soon,' Taj Mohammad added.

'What choice do we have? If we remain here it's a matter of time before we are overrun. If we take advantage of the air attack there is a slim possibility that we may succeed in reaching Top. Once we are on Top, it is between the enemy and us—and let the best man win. I would rather die attacking than waiting for them to overrun us. It's probably our best chance and perhaps the most honourable thing to do.'

Hamir had shared his views in the only way he knew— simply, directly and without mincing his words.

Before either Gosain or Taj Mohammad could respond, Hari Singh's voice could be heard on Gosain's radio set.

'Charlie, air attack has been allotted for Top. Time on target is 11:30 hours. Prepare for attack.'

'Charlie, wilco,' Hamir replied.

Now the Pakistani radio operator who had been listening in jumped in to add his remarks.

'Charlie, have you gone mad? You are heading for certain death. Take my word. Surrender now, or prepare to meet your maker.'

Hamir looked towards his operator and shushed him quiet. He was not sure whether the enemy operator had heard the plan or not, but what he said was actually true. As per the new plan they *were* heading for certain death.

'Sahab, yeh to Jan Jorah raid se bhi badtar plan hai. Sirf is baar hum wapas nahin aa payenge!' Taj Mohammad said wryly. *Sir, this plan is worse than the Jan Jorah raid. Only this time there will be no coming back!*

Taj Mohammad was referring to a raid Hamir's company had been tasked to carry out a few days after the war had commenced. *How I wish there was a better reading of the ground*, Hamir lamented. Notwithstanding the proposed use of aircraft, a charge on Top in broad daylight would in all probability be as futile as that raid had been. For a moment his mind wandered to the events of the ninth of December.

9 December 1971. Battalion HQ

'Here, take a look,' Inderjit pointed on the map with his pencil. 'This is village Jan Jorah and this is the area where the enemy guns are believed to be deployed.' On the map the area appeared to be a relatively flat piece of ground with adequate space to deploy a battery of artillery guns.

'Yes, sir. Seen,' Hamir replied.

'It's just on the outskirts of Jan Jorah village. This is your platoon's target,' Inderjit declared. 'I am sure you will replicate Khan's success. Please work out your plan soon. The platoon needs to leave this evening and return by tomorrow morning.'

'Tomorrow morning?' Hamir replied, surprised. 'Sir, it won't be possible. They will need an extra night. It's almost eight kilometres on the map. And take a look at the contours. On the way out the platoon will need to go through our own minefields, then down the steep slope of OP Hill, cross the nala, locate the guns and then destroy them. On the way back, they need to return to the nala, get across it, climb up OP Hill and return through our own minefields. OP Hill in itself is a challenging three to four hour climb in normal times. You can imagine how much time the entire operation will take.'

'But Khan's company returned by morning, after destroying the Atian supply point,' Inderjit interjected.

'That was on the next ridgeline, sir. One could see it from Pir Badesar. Jan Jorah is way inside and no one knows exactly where the guns are!' Hamir remarked. 'The entire operation won't take less than eighteen to twenty hours!'

'C'mon, Hamir. I am sure your guys can do it, just give it a try. If need be, you go along with them.'

'Sure, sir, I will. But I think you need to inform the brigade that we need more time. Also, I will accompany the platoon,' Hamir suggested.

'You leave that to me. Just prepare to leave immediately after last light. You will have Gosain as your FOO and an engineer officer who will handle the explosives to destroy the guns. See you at the start point in the evening.'

Hamir was astonished. *How could there be such a poor understanding of the ground?* He was fortunate to have spent his formative years in Ladakh and NEFA where he had learnt to read the map and recognize the peculiarities of such terrain.

Delta Company's raid on the supply point at Atian on 7 December 1971 had been a resounding success. Khan had led his company well and Inderjit was proud of the success achieved. But Hamir's task was vastly different. Atian was not too far away from Pir Badesar and its exact location was known. What is more, the battery of guns reported near village Jan Jorah would have to be located first to enable their destruction.

Success at Atian seemed to have made Lt Col Inderjit somewhat overconfident. Whether he conveyed Hamir's reservations about the raid to the brigade commander or not was not certain but Hamir received a go-ahead. The raid was to be launched from the Indian picket of OP Hill in the Mendhar Sector. Inderjit saw them off as they left OP Hill immediately after last light.

The first leg of the raid itself took longer than expected. The minefield guides were extremely circumspect and it took them over an hour to get through the gaps in the Indian minefields. Movement down the steep slope of OP Hill and the dense jungle proved extremely difficult. By the time they reached the base of the mountain and crossed the nala it was already 01:00 hours. Realizing that they were well short of the objective the operation was called off and the platoon was asked to return immediately.

Now it was a race against time. They had only about five hours to daylight and if day lighted they would be easy pickings for the enemy located on the enemy picket facing OP Hill. The platoon got across the nala in good time and rushed up OP Hill as fast as they could. The final hurdle was getting through the minefield, which they did just as day was breaking.

The Jan Jorah raid was a needless exercise attributable to theoretical off-the-map planning and poor understanding of the terrain. The only saving grace was that the operation had been called off in time due to which lives had been saved.

~

Back on the SW Spur of Daruchhian, time was ticking. It was 11:15 hours and they had about fifteen minutes before the commencement of the air attack.

'Excuse me, sir, what's the plan now?' Gosain's voice quickly brought back Hamir to the situation at West Spur.

He quickly gathered his thoughts. The last stretch of 150–200 yards to Top was rocky and provided no cover. It was nearly noon and the visibility being excellent the men would be exposed for the entire duration of the assault. Given the circumstances there was not much to plan.

What has to be done has to be done, Hamir concluded. He made a simple plan and shared it with Gosain and Taj Mohammad.

All available men would be split into two groups. One would assault Top while the other would take on the enemy company approaching their position for a counterattack.

'I will lead the first group going for Top with Captain Gosain and Alam Ali's platoon. Taj Mohammad sahab, you will command the group responsible for holding the enemy coming from below,' Hamir explained. 'They should not be able to interfere in our attack. As soon as Top is captured, I shall give you the signal. Your group should then join us at Top,' he added.

After he had finished, Taj Mohammad walked up to Hamir and said, 'Sahab, can I have a word with you?'

'Sure, sahab, what is it?' Hamir replied.

'Sahab, you plan to lead the assault… Your wounds don't allow you to even hold a weapon in your hands. How do you propose to take on the enemy?'

'Taj Mohammad sahab, I realize that we are in a hopeless situation and there is absolutely no chance of survival,' Hamir replied. 'How can I order my men to certain death, without joining them? Let me have the opportunity to die with them. I will lead, come what may,' he added.

He then placed his hand on Taj Mohammad's shoulder—'I am fortunate to have a comrade like you. Apna dhyan rakhna, sahab.' *Be careful, look after yourself.* 'Khuda hafiz, Jai Hind.'

Hamir left no room for further discussion. As they bid farewell to each other, Hamir hugged Taj Mohammad. He had been the company's rock and had stuck with him through thick and thin.

'May Allah protect you, sahab. Inshallah, we shall meet on Top,' Taj Mohammad remarked. As he turned away, Hamir could catch the sadness in Taj Mohammad's eyes. It was an emotional moment as they realized it was probably their final meeting.

Both groups dispersed to their respective areas to take up their positions. All that was left to be done was to wait for the aircrafts to bomb Daruchhian Top.

Exactly at 11:30 hours the sound of approaching aircraft could be heard in the distance. The first wave of aircraft was arriving on the target. The air attack on Top had commenced.

The aircraft would attack in three waves, which implied Hamir had about five minutes before commencing the ground attack.

The sun was nearly overhead as Hamir looked around to see his men. They seemed ready. Some of them were resting with their eyes closed, while others were immersed in prayer, silently reciting the Quran. It was a surreal scene, almost as if he was watching a movie. He undid the button of his shirt pocket and took out its precious contents. He glanced at the photos of his family for a final time.

Sapana, I did my very best. I leave you, Vikram and Vijay in God's hands. Farewell.

The second wave of aircraft flew over their heads, strafing the enemy positions.

Thinking of his father, he said, *I hope I make you proud, Papa!*

The third and final wave of aircraft flew over their heads attacking the enemy positions.

'Charlie, that's it. Go for it. Godspeed,' Brigadier Hari Singh had given the final go-ahead. Hamir stood up and waved to his men to start moving.

His team of thirty-odd men emerged from their positions and aligned themselves towards the objective. They crouched in an extended line about a metre or two apart. Hamir began climbing the slope. Taking cue, his men began moving as well, firing their weapons as they climbed the final stretch of 150 yards to Daruchhian Top.

The enemy on Top had a clear view of the advancing Indians and greeted them with a heavy volume of fire. Simultaneously, artillery fire opened up.

The shell that knocked Hamir down fell about twenty yards behind him. Had the large boulders in the area not shielded him Hamir would have definitely lost his life. The hand of providence indeed! The terrifying blast in such close proximity was, however, good enough to knock him cold.

~

'Sahab…sahab ji…'

The voice was weak, almost faint and in some distress. The words, however, sounded familiar. They could have been spoken either by one of his men, or Laxmi.

Whether it was the voice of one of his men or Laxmi didn't really matter. He loved them both equally and, therefore, the words demanded his immediate attention.

'Haan, kaun?' he muttered, opening his eyes. *Who is it?* He glanced in the direction of the source of the sound—whether it was the voice of a man or a woman, strangely, he doesn't remember.

To his surprise there was no one to be seen. But then the voice had been very real. He was now a bit confused; to make matters worse he had no recollection of where he was. It was mid morning and he could feel the warmth of the morning sun. But what was he doing lying out in the open, tucked uncomfortably amid a pair of large boulders?

He glanced to his left and then to his right. Not finding anyone or anything familiar, he turned his head to look behind him. He was stunned by what he saw. The body of a soldier lay in a bizarre position, a position possible only in death.

The shock of seeing his dead colleague instantly brought him back to reality—he had been knocked down by the blast of a near-miss artillery shell. His objective, Daruchhian Top, was still about 150 yards away. As he contemplated his next move his father's words echoed in his head—'Son, I can bear your loss, but not disgrace!'

Under intense enemy fire, Hamir stood up, adjusting his heavily bandaged right arm into its sling over his damp blood-soaked shirt. Seeing him get back on his feet, his men followed, standing abreast, rifles in their hands. Hamir hung his personal weapon on his back. It was of little use now; he had lost the use of his firing arm. *I am afraid you will have to live with my loss, Papa.* 'Sarvada Shaktishali,' he yelled, and was off, leading his band of thirty-odd soldiers to their destiny, as the enemy beckoned from Daruchhian Top.

They started off slowly, a few yards at a time, moving from fire position to fire position. The intensity of enemy fire increased as they advanced up the slope. To dodge the bullets they would dash across open spaces and crawl when required. Right in front was Hamir, who led the men, oblivious to the fire. He had resigned himself to the inevitable burst which would cut him down, ending his battle and his life.

He was now just seventy-five yards from the concrete bunkers of Top. When he looked around searching for his comrades he realized that he was alone—in the open and slightly ahead of the others. He needed to wait at an appropriate place to allow the others to close in. His eyes fell upon a large boulder, approximately fifty yards ahead. *That would do just fine*, he decided. He set off immediately, zigzagging through the automatic fire until he reached the rock and lay down behind it. After about five minutes the firing stopped.

'Ibrahim...Ibrahim...' Hamir whispered loudly. His operator should have been next to him by now. There was no response. He tried again, a bit louder. 'Ibrahim...Ibrahim...' This time he heard some movement towards his left.

As Hamir turned he found an unfamiliar soldier looking curiously at him. He was dressed in khakis in contrast to Hamir's olive green. They stared at each for a few seconds, frozen with the surreality of facing one's enemy at close proximity.

The Pakistani soldier lifted his Sten gun and aimed at Hamir, who had no weapon. Instinctively Hamir shut his eyes and raised his left hand to protect his face, bracing for the burst. *That's it, I am done for*, Hamir thought.

The burst from the enemy's Sten gun was loud as he had fired from just fifteen yards away. The bullets whizzed past Hamir's face. The nervous Pakistani had missed.

Hamir opened his eyes only to find the Pakistani soldier aiming at him a second time. The soldier pressed the trigger again. This time, however, there was no fire, just a loud metallic sound. The weapon had malfunctioned. Hamir had cheated death yet again.

This was the opportunity he had been waiting for. He got up immediately to rush the Pakistani soldier who now in panic yelled aloud, 'Pakdo, pakdo!' *Catch him, catch him!*

Two Pakistani soldiers, armed with bayonet-fixed rifles, suddenly appeared from the trenches on the right and jumped upon Hamir. He was pinned to the ground, unable to move.

The soldier who had fired rushed towards Hamir in anger. He had caused them a lot of trouble. He grabbed at Hamir's collar, ready to strike him with his fist, when his eyes fell on his epaulets. He was taken aback. Till then he hadn't realized that Hamir was an officer. Instinctively he released his collar. 'Arre! Aap to sahab hain!' he remarked, surprised. *Oh! You are an officer!* He sounded embarrassed; the need to respect all officers had been ingrained in him.

'Let's take him to the bunker, fire is about to commence,' the other soldiers suggested. Apparently the battle was still on.

They helped Hamir onto his feet and drag-pushed him into a nearby LMG bunker. The bunker had overhead protection and allowed observation and fire.

They had just entered the bunker when the firing resumed. Hamir could see his men reaching Top in ones and twos, only to be shot or forced down the hill.

'Look, look, sir. Your men are running away like rats, we have got them on the run,' the Pakistani soldier remarked gleefully. That was the last Hamir saw of his men.

He remained in the bunker with his captors until the firing stopped. At about 12:00 hours he was escorted towards Mule Shed on the lower slopes of the feature, about 300 yards away. *Why are they taking me to Mule Shed?* he wondered. On reaching Mule Shed he was shepherded into an abandoned village hut which had been converted into a regimental aid post (RAP). He realized that what they had been referring to as Mule Shed all along was actually an RAP.

A number of wounded Pakistani soldiers were sitting outside the RAP hut. The moment they saw Hamir they were livid.

'Why have you got him alive? The pig deserves to die; he's killed so many of us. Just kill him right now!'

The Army Medical Corps JCO at the RAP realized that the situation was getting dangerous. He needed to be quick. He tore open Hamir's shirt sleeve and rendered him first aid as fast as he could.

'Sir, I suggest you just remain silent and wait here. I can't guarantee your safety if you leave this hut.'

Hamir realized what the man was saying was absolutely true. He had received a very hostile reception outside the RAP, he wouldn't like to be left to them. As the JCO locked the door Hamir sat down on the bed, silently staring at the door. *My war is over*, he thought. It wasn't long before fatigue got the better of him and he dozed off.

~

Hamir was woken up by the loud shouting outside his door.

'Major sahab aa gaye hain, darwaza kholo!' someone shouted. *The Major has arrived. Unlock the door.*

The Pakistani Medical JCO unlocked the door and pushed it open. A Pakistani major was standing outside. He looked at Hamir, while the Medical JCO informed the major about the bullet injuries that Hamir had suffered on his right hand. He confirmed that the prisoner had no injuries below his waist. The major nodded. He then turned his attention towards Hamir and said, 'How are you?'

'I am fine,' Hamir replied.

'Can you walk?'

'Yes.'

'OK, then please come down with me. I can't leave you here. As you can see, you are not welcome here.'

Looking at the JCO who had captured Hamir, the major remarked, 'Sahab, you needn't worry now. I will take him with me.' The JCO saluted as the major led Hamir down the slopes of Daruchhian, escorted by four soldiers.

'So what's your name?' the major asked.

'Hamir Singh.'

'Oh, I see! Singh—so you are a Sikh?'

'No. I am a Rajput,' Hamir clarified.

'Achha, achha! Matlab Rajputana se ho?' he concluded. *OK! That means you are from Rajputana?*

It took Hamir some time to understand that he meant Rajasthan.

'Yes, that's correct,' Hamir replied.

'You know, I am also a Bhati Rajput. Our ancestors belonged to Jodhpur in Rajputana. They accompanied Raja Jaswant Singh to battle in Afghanistan and then remained there, converting to Islam later.'

The major continued talking with Hamir as they walked on a track amidst the fields beside the Poonch River. They had been walking for almost an hour when they reached the bridge that Bhagwan's platoon was to have secured. There were a number of Pakistani vehicles standing across the bridge. The major led Hamir to an ambulance.

'OK, please get into the ambulance, it will take you further. I will need to take leave now. All the best!' That was the last he saw of the major.

The medical staff helped Hamir into the ambulance and it was soon on its way. Their journey was about an hour long and when the vehicle arrived at its destination, it was late evening.

A young doctor helped Hamir out and escorted him to a medical shelter. His wounds were tended to after which he was asked to remain seated until further orders. After some time a Pakistani subedar major (SM) entered the shelter and informed Hamir that he was to meet the commanding officer who was waiting in his office. *If the CO is stationed here, this must be the HQ of the battalion*, Hamir assumed.

'Let's go, sir,' the subedar major remarked. As Hamir stood up to follow him, the subedar major noticed that he was without a blindfold.

'Oh! These people have forgotten to blindfold you!' he remarked. He picked up a spare bandage from the doctor's table and tightly bound it over Hamir's eyes.

Now that he was blindfolded the subedar major helped Hamir find his way. He could sense that he was being escorted down a flight of stairs, probably into an underground bunker. The room was warm and the sound of typewriters could be heard in the background. *I am in the CO's office*, Hamir thought.

'So, Commando, how are you?' someone called out. The voice belonged to a man of authority. *It must be the CO*, Hamir presumed. *But why is he calling me a commando?*

'I am fine, thank you,' Hamir replied.

'Since last night we have been repeatedly telling you to surrender, but no, you wouldn't listen! Why didn't you just surrender? Would have saved us a great deal of bother. Besides, you wouldn't have been in this situation!' the man remarked.

'I was just following the orders of my CO!' Hamir said.

'What's your name?'

'Hamir Singh.'

'Sikh, eh?'

'No, sir. Rajput,' Hamir replied.

'Oho...Rajput! So that's the reason. Shahadat qubool karoge, ita'at nahin!' he commented. *You'd rather embrace martyrdom than surrender!*

Hamir didn't reply. The CO conversed with Hamir for some more time until his curiosity was satisfied.

'OK, there's nothing more to be done, SM sahab, take him away.' Hamir could hear him stand up. 'But, young man, your CO would be proud of you! You fought well.'

The subedar major escorted Hamir to an adjacent room, where he left him under the watchful eyes of a sentry.

It was a chilly winter evening and Hamir was hungry and cold. He hadn't eaten a morsel for a very long time and he wasn't adequately clothed. Although he wore a warm overcoat he had only a vest under it. His woollen shirt had been ripped apart while being treated for his wounds. The sentry must have noticed him shivering. He left the room for a moment and returned with a hot mug of tea which Hamir gratefully accepted.

'Here, sir, let me help you wear this kurta, you will feel better,' he said. The good man had apparently brought something for Hamir to wear. He helped Hamir remove the overcoat and put on the shirt which, thanks to his heavily bandaged hand, was a challenge in itself. But on wearing the kurta Hamir definitely felt better and his shivering stopped.

He waited in the room lost in his thoughts, wondering what the future had in store for him. After a while the SM returned and informed Hamir that it was time to move.

'Right, sir, we need to leave. You are being sent to the rear,' he said. 'Rear' implied that he was now moving away from the battlefront.

Still blindfolded, his escort led him out of the bunker and into a waiting truck. As he took his seat in the driver's cabin, he could feel the presence of men sitting on either side of him. The SM had a word of advice for his escorts.

'Daroga sahab, dhyan rakhna,' he said. *Daroga sahab, you'd better be careful.* 'He's a commando,' he added. 'He may seem injured but that doesn't mean he can't sort you out. You better remain alert!'

'Daroga' in most parts of India and Pakistan is a term used to address policemen. *So now I am in police custody*, Hamir figured.

The policeman rechecked Hamir's handcuff for the umpteenth time. After making sure that his handcuffed hand was securely anchored to the body of the vehicle the Daroga ordered the driver to start the vehicle. The engine stirred to life and they were soon on their way. The driver's cabin was small; Hamir sat cramped in between the driver and the Daroga.

Crime wasn't much of an issue near the border regions. Normally the 'Daroga sahab' would escort no more than an odd petty criminal. Here he was escorting an Indian commando whose physical presence itself was nerve-racking. Due to the limited space the Daroga's body brushed involuntarily against Hamir as the vehicle moved. Hamir could feel the nervous policeman shudder from time to time. Luckily for the policeman the journey wasn't too long and they reached their destination in about two hours.

Hamir was helped to disembark from the vehicle and escorted into what felt like a prison cell. He was then asked to sit down on an uncomfortable cement platform. The stench of the cell was unbearable; it was evident that the toilet had not been cleaned in a long time. Though tired, it was impossible for him to sleep in the suffocating environment. He drifted in and out of sleep until he was woken up by the sound of movement within the premises and someone shouting aloud. 'GMP aa gayi hai. Qaidi ko taiyar karo!' *The GMP has arrived. Prepare the prisoner!*

The announcement implied that the GMP (Garrison Military Police) from the nearest army garrison was now taking charge of Hamir. He was escorted out of the cell and led into a military jeep. As he was being handed over, Hamir heard the Daroga remark in relief, 'Lo ji, sambhalo apne commando ko! Ab aap jaano our aapka kaam jaane!' *OK now, take charge of your commando. He's all yours now!*

'Haan, haan, koi gal nai, Daroga sahab, aap aaraam karo,' the GMP personnel replied in Punjabi, laughing. *Yes, yes, Daroga sahab, now you relax.*

~

This time their journey was very short and they reached the garrison in about fifteen to twenty minutes. Hamir was led into a room, where finally, after almost twelve hours, his blindfold was removed.

He looked around inquisitively. He was in some sort of army medical facility and the staff were busy attending to the wounded. On seeing Hamir, a major from the Army Medical Corps, walked up to him.

'How are you feeling?' he inquired.

'I am OK,' Hamir replied.

'Let me have a look at you,' the major first glanced through Hamir's papers, after which he examined his injuries.

'It says here you are Major Hamir Singh.'

'Yes, that's correct.'

'From where?'

'Rajasthan.'

'OK. I belong to Uttar Pradesh. I studied medicine at King George's Medical College, Lucknow.'

Hamir smiled.

'Your wounds seem fine. Any pain?'

'No.'

'OK, we need to take some X-rays to see the damage to your bones,' he announced.

He gestured to the nursing assistant who took him to the neighbouring room. The X-ray was done in a few minutes and handed over to the doctor. He looked at it for a few minutes trying to assess the damage Hamir's hand had suffered.

'You are lucky. The bullet has gone through the upper arm damaging the bone, which remained stuck to the muscle. Without any bone we would have no option but to amputate your hand,' he said. 'Now we have something to work on. I think we can sort this out. We will start the process immediately,' he added. 'Is that OK?'

'Yes, I guess so,' Hamir replied.

'Great, you sure are a tough guy, Major,' the doctor remarked. 'Please prepare him for the operation,' he ordered the staff.

As he lay on his bed and the staff attended to him, the doctor's words remained in his thoughts. Hamir was reminded of the time when as a second lieutenant with 2 Grenadiers he had been addressed as a 'tough guy'. It was in Ladakh, back in the winter of 1963.

January 1963. Ladakh

'Tough guy, eh?' Major S.R. Das was dressing Hamir down. 'Young man, I hope you know there's a saying around this place—"Don't be a Gama in the Land of Lama!"[14] Hereafter, you will *always* follow the rules, Mr Hamir. You understand?' When Das was really angry he would always address the person he was angry with as Mister.

'Yes, sir!' Hamir barked out loudly in military cadet fashion.

Hamir had recently been commissioned into 2 Grenadiers in December 1962. The just concluded Sino-Indian War had resulted in the mobilization of troops into Ladakh and 2 Grenadiers had been airlifted and deployed at Leh Airport. Hamir was posted into Delta Company which was deployed on a hill just across the airport. After the initial acclimatization his company was asked to proceed to Karu. The conditions were tough and accommodation spartan. Hamir had only a tent to sleep in and since it was December the nights were extremely cold. Snowfall had already begun and the area was covered with six to nine inches of snow.

To ensure good health strict guidelines had been laid down for the men. The rules stipulated that no one was to leave their accommodation prior to 09:00 hours in the morning. Similarly, in the evening all activities would cease at 15:00 hours, after which every soldier was expected to return to their living accommodation.

Following these instructions for the first few days had

bored a young, physically active Hamir. Early one morning he decided to embark on an impromptu stroll around the mountainside. Panic gripped the others when they awoke to find Hamir missing. Search parties were dispatched in all directions. Finally, after spending many hours looking for the young officer, he was found casually climbing down the mountain, returning from his little expedition.

The company senior JCO was obviously furious and admonished the youngster. The matter was reported to their company commander Major Das who was equally livid, making Hamir the ire of his anger.

Hamir had learnt his lesson. He realized that his carelessness had risked the lives of the men who had spent many hours searching for him. Thereafter he strictly adhered to the rules, curtailing his natural instincts. His boredom and frustration reflected on his face, and to an experienced Major Das, it was more than obvious that Hamir needed some diversion.

Therefore, when his company was tasked to construct defences at the higher reaches near Karu, Major Das immediately assigned him the job. Hamir was more than eager and took to it like duck to water.

To reach the area selected for the construction they would need to undertake a brisk climb of an hour or so every morning. On reaching the location Hamir would move from bunker to bunker supervising the work enthusiastically, until it was time for them to climb down to their camp site.

During the lunch break one day Hamir noticed some birds on the ridge-line approximately 100 yards away. He had never seen such birds before. In appearance they looked like partridges but their behaviour was akin to pigeons. They were in fact chakors.

On seeing the chakors, Hamir recollected the conversation during dinner the previous night. Major Das had drunk more than his normal quota of rum.

'Hamir, if you really are as tough as you look, why don't you get me some bloody non-vegetarian stuff? I am sick of this infernal dal and potatoes!' Das had remarked.

It was hard to tell if Das really meant it or whether it was said in jest. Hamir, though, replied like a good soldier.

'Yes, sir. I shall definitely do that,' he said.

Since they were located at a remote high-altitude location their survival was based on canned food or dry rations which included a generous amount of dal and potatoes. For a thoroughbred Bengali managing without non-vegetarian dishes for an extended period had been especially tough.

When Hamir saw the well-fed chakors he was convinced that the Almighty had heard the prayers of Major Das. He picked up his .303 rifle and aimed at the birds. Generally a good shot, possibly due to altitude, the cold climate or the excitement, Hamir had to fire almost thirty to forty rounds before he got his first kill. Four rounds later he had his second.

Dinner that day was a celebration of life with much backslapping and happy banter. Das was full of praise for this enterprising youngster.

Thereafter Hamir's hunting forays became a regular feature. He saw in it an opportunity to train his soldiers on the basics of marksmanship. Some of his men were to attend weapons courses in the near future and for them it was a good practical opportunity to hone their skills. As for Das, he had all the non-vegetarian food he craved. It was, however, a secret zealously guarded by the company.

A few months later Major Das proceeded on leave, after which he was posted out. With no replacement available Hamir was appointed as the officiating company commander.

Hamir enjoyed his job tremendously. He was forever on the move, scaling the peaks around the area. During one such trek, while returning to camp Hamir found a group of wild goats near a water body in the valley below. Since it was already late in the evening he did not venture towards them and returned home. However, he made a mental note of the location and decided he would return at an appropriate time after discussing it with his local friend, philosopher and guide, Norbu.

With Norbu (to Hamir's left) and his family, many years after the events described in this book.

Norbu, a young lad, about sixteen years old, was an enterprising and resourceful local lad. He belonged to the Igoo village near Karu. Though formally educated up to class five only, he was a multifaceted individual. He could converse in Hindi and served both as an interpreter as well as a supplier of horses whenever required by the army for administrative purposes. For Hamir he served as a willing volunteer in all his ventures.

Early morning on the following Sunday, Hamir, accompanied by a team of two soldiers and Norbu, headed for an impromptu safari to hunt for wild goats.

Since it was a long trek Hamir decided to travel the first leg of the journey in a one ton vehicle. Thereafter they would travel the rest of the distance on foot. The vehicle dropped them at the designated place. Hamir asked the driver to head back for the camp and return to pick them up at the same place at four in the evening.

They walked up to the area and after a couple of hours were successful in getting their first wild goat. It was a handsome male specimen with a large head and an impressive pair of horns. He weighed about forty to fifty kilograms.

By the time they reached the designated pick-up location it was way past four. The driver had waited for an hour and as it was getting dark he rushed back to inform his senior JCO that the officiating company commander hadn't returned. The JCO immediately ordered him back to the pick-up location with orders that even if he had to spend the night there he would remain waiting.

Meanwhile, unfortunately for the company, the commanding officer Lieutenant Colonel J. Nazareth decided to make an unannounced visit to Hamir's company. When he reached the company he found him missing. The senior JCO informed him that Hamir had left in the morning to carry out a reconnaissance of the area. He would return shortly. The CO seemed satisfied and retired to his room for dinner.

The driver waited for Hamir nervously, quite in a quandary, unsure whether he should wait or return. The senior JCO too was equally worried. Not only did he have no idea where Hamir was, he wouldn't be able to send a search party before the next morning either.

Hamir and his partner returned to their pick-up point at about seven o'clock to the relief of the driver waiting for him. The dead goat was placed in the vehicle and they returned to their base.

On reaching the company Hamir reported to Nazareth. He briefed him about his so-called 'reconnaissance mission'. Later at an appropriate time he slipped in his 'coincidental' encounter with the wild goat and its inevitable death.

The CO was already impressed by the young officer's devotion to duty; after all he had taken the initiative of carrying out a recce mission despite it being a Sunday. But when he heard of the hunt he was absolutely thrilled.

He insisted on seeing the dead animal immediately. He was taken to the vehicle in which the poor beast lay. Nazareth delighted, grinned with pleasure and thumped Hamir's back.

'Well done, my boy!' he said. 'I am really proud of you. I must inform the Brigade Commander immediately.'

The news was conveyed to the brigade commander, who in turn informed the GOC.

Here was a young officer who instead of worrying about the tough conditions had been patrolling the hills with a sense of duty. He was even enterprising enough to find a wild goat and skilled enough to bring it down. All these were seen as desirable qualities in any young officer.

Hamir was now well known in the entire division and after a few days he was asked to report to the Division HQ where the GOC would meet him.

The meeting was cordial. Maj Gen Budh Singh had seen service as a jawan in 2 Grenadiers before he became an officer and held the battalion in high regard. He was happy to meet Hamir and complimented him for his adventurous spirit and physical toughness. They conversed for some time about routine matters.

A few days later, Lt Col Nazareth summoned Hamir to the Battalion HQ and said, 'Hamir, I would like to participate in a wild goat hunt. Let's go out tomorrow.'

'Definitely, sir. It will be my pleasure,' Hamir replied, a bit surprised by the request.

When they left the next morning, Hamir's hunting party included the CO and a few selected men. They headed for the same area where Hamir had seen the goats earlier.

After a few hours Hamir spotted a few wild goats which had come down for a drink to the rivulet at the bottom of the valley. They were more than 200 yards away. Hamir asked the rest of the party to halt on the track lest the goats run away. He walked ahead alone and shot at them from approximately 100 yards. As he fired the sound of his gun echoed throughout the valley and the goats scampered in panic. One goat was killed instantaneously and fell near the rivulet, while a second, only injured, started climbing up the mountain on the other side of the rivulet. Seeing the wounded goat Hamir took off in its direction.

'Where are you going?' Nazareth yelled.

'Sir, one of them is not dead yet. Can't leave him injured, I will get him,' Hamir said, as he took off in the direction of the goat. In a short while both Hamir and the goat were out of sight.

It had been quite a while since Hamir had disappeared. Worried, the CO looked at his watch nervously while the rest of the party scanned the mountainside looking for the youngster. Hamir had left alone and there was no way one could contact him. *I hope he is fine*, the CO prayed.

A few moments later soldiers excitedly pointed towards Hamir, whose frame was now visible on the mountain, silhouetted against the sky, 300 metres away. Draped over his shoulders was the carcass of a huge goat. After another thirty minutes he was back with the hunting party. Tired, he dropped the massive beast at the feet of his CO. Visibly impressed, he hugged Hamir warmly and remarked, 'Well done, young man. You sure are one tough guy!'

~

Back in the Pakistani forward medical facility Hamir's pre-operation formalities had been completed. He was asked to lie down on the operating table, given a couple of injections and administered anaesthesia. His last memory before losing consciousness was looking for his purse which contained the precious photos of his family.

Part Two
THE ROAD TO RECOVERY

The chirping of the birds awakened Hamir. He felt well rested and snug in a comfortable set of linen and blankets. His back hurt probably since, heavily drugged, he had remained on his back throughout the night. He turned to his side looking towards the window through which the morning light filtered into the room. His movement alerted someone in the room. He could hear the person rush out of the room and return with the doctor.

'How are you feeling today, Major Hamir Singh?' Hamir recognized the voice. It was the Pakistani army doctor who had attended to him the previous day.

'I feel fine, thank you, doctor,' Hamir replied.

'So the good news is that the operation went well,' the doctor remarked. 'You are doing fine. It should take approximately four to six weeks for the wounds to heal. Later the upper arm may need another operation.'

'OK,' Hamir replied.

'There is not much more we can do for you here. We will evacuate you to a new location where you will be able to recuperate.'

The Pakistani doctor left the room, only to return five minutes later.

'Major Hamir, before you leave, I have a request. Would you be comfortable meeting some ladies?'

'Ladies?' Hamir responded, surprised. *Who in the world would want to meet me here, in Pakistan? Is this some kind of interrogation technique they are attempting?* he wondered.

'Sure, it's fine with me,' Hamir replied, confused. He couldn't wait to find out who the ladies were. In any case, meeting them would surely do him no harm.

'Thank you. Then I will just get them in.'

The doctor went out and returned with two women. They looked young and were dressed in traditional wear. They stood silently for some time, observing Hamir. Finally the younger one gathered courage and spoke up.

'I believe you have an injury,' she said.

'Yes, that's correct,' Hamir replied.

'Where are you hurt?'

Hamir removed his right hand from under the blanket and held it up. He thought he saw a hint of a grimace in her expression.

'Dard hota hai kya?' the older lady spoke this time. *Does it hurt?*

'No, not really.'

'Kya aap shadi-shuda hain?' *Are you married?*

'Ji,' Hamir nodded.

Hamir wondered whether he was being interrogated or if they really were just inquisitive local women. *No use letting my guard down*, he thought. His replies were brief and to the point, although he answered respectfully without sounding impolite. The ladies were now reasonably comfortable speaking to him.

'Do you have children?' the younger one asked.

'Yes, I have two boys.'

'Where are they?'

'They are with my wife, at her father's place,' Hamir replied.

'Do you miss them?' the older lady interjected.

Hamir did not reply. He hadn't really had time to think of his family. His facial expression changed. The ladies realized that their question had made him uncomfortable. They quickly changed the topic.

'Hum aapke liye keenu laye hain!' the older lady said. *We have bought some kinnow for you to eat.*

Hamir had never heard the word 'keenu' before. He looked confused.

'We mean oranges,' the younger one clarified. 'Will you accept our oranges?'

Hamir nodded, he had no reason to refuse. Pleased, the ladies fumbled through their bag and took out a few oranges and placed them on his bedside table.

'Here, please have them,' they offered.

The citrus orange-like fruit looked and smelled delicious but Hamir made no attempt to eat them.

'You are not eating them,' the young one observed.

'Because I can't peel them,' he replied and raised his bandaged right hand to their amusement. He could hear them giggle.

'Hum chheelenge to kya aap kha lenge?' *Will you eat them if we peel them for you?*

'Kyun nahin?' Hamir replied. *Why not?*

'Kyunki hum Musalman hain!' they spoke almost in unison. *Because we are Muslim!*

'How does that matter?' Hamir queried.

'We thought you may not like to eat from the hands of a Muslim.'

Hamir was surprised. They seemed to have some strange perception about Hindus.

'I have no such problem. My company consisted of Muslim men. We often ate together,' he explained.

'Oh! We were under the impression…' They didn't care to finish the sentence, embarrassed at their assumption. They peeled the remaining oranges silently, placing them one by one on a plate.

Hamir picked up the oranges, separated their segments and carefully placed them in his mouth. They were juicy and delicious. The ladies were happy to see him savour their little gift. After some time the older one spoke up.

'I think we should go now. We enjoyed interacting with you. May God be with you. Khuda hafiz.'

'Khuda hafiz, and thank you for the oranges, they were really delicious,' Hamir smiled as they left his room. He had enjoyed meeting the two ladies. Though unexpected, it had been a pleasant interaction.

Later in the afternoon the Pakistani doctor returned.

'Thank you for agreeing to meet the ladies. They have never met an Indian soldier in real life. It has been a unique experience for them.'

'I can understand,' Hamir replied.

'OK, Major. It's now time for you to leave. You will be escorted out of this hospital. Before you leave a few correspondents from Radio Pakistan will interact with you.'

'Will that be necessary?' Hamir asked.

'Yes. It will be good for you as once they get your particulars they will make an announcement about your capture and well-being on the radio. I am sure your people are anxiously waiting for news about you,' the doctor replied. What he said made sense.

'Right, I understand,' Hamir acknowledged.

'All the best, Major. Inshallah, you will be fine soon,' the doctor smiled as he bid farewell to Hamir.

The medical staff blindfolded Hamir before wheeling him out to a waiting ambulance. A crowd had gathered near the ambulance and as Hamir's stretcher closed in the crowd began jostling to get a glimpse of the Indian prisoner. Hamir could hear the unmistakable sounds of movie cameras and camera flashes. He was soon subjected to a barrage of questions from the journalists.

—'What's your name?'
—'Where were you captured?'
—'Are you married?'
—'What injury do you have? Are you OK?'

Hamir remained silent. Someone accompanying him answered the questions on his behalf. The exchange continued for quite some time until his escorts decided that it was time to leave.

'OK, you have had enough time. Move aside, we need to leave right now!'

This had the desired effect on the journalists. They quietened down and dispersed. Hamir's stretcher was now hauled into the body of the ambulance. In a short while he was on the next leg of his journey in Pakistan.

~

The Road to Recovery

They must have been travelling for the better part of the night. A combination of the swaying of the vehicle and the effect of medication ensured he slept soundly. It was only when the engine of the ambulance was switched off did Hamir realize that he had actually slept through the journey. He could hear the sound of footsteps as someone approached the vehicle.

'How many people inside?' It was a female voice.

'Only one, a major. A large, moustached commando!'

'Achha? Abhi dekhti hoon is muchhadd ko!' she remarked. *Oh, I see! Let me have a look at him.* The lady had a loud matron-like voice.

'Chalo, ab darwaza toh kholo!' she ordered. *Go on, open the door now!*

The ambulance's door was opened and Hamir's stretcher eased out. Hamir, still blindfolded, had no idea where he was or who was barking the orders.

'So this is your commando!' the lady remarked. She now seemed somewhat subdued. The sight of Hamir probably mellowed her down.

'Take him inside,' she ordered.

The stretcher was placed on a wheeled trolley and pushed until they reached a room. The helpers lifted him from the stretcher and placed him on a comfortable hospital bed.

'Commando, are you OK?' the lady inquired.

'Yes, I am fine,' Hamir replied.

'Aur tum kaise ho, Jawan?' she continued. *And how are you, soldier?*

Hamir realized that there was someone else in the room whom the nurse was now addressing.

'I am OK, madam,' the voice sounded familiar. It sounded like his company havildar major.

'Asif?' Hamir queried.

'Sahab!' replied the surprised soldier.

'Shh, chupp. Yahan baat-cheet ki ijazat nahin hai!' the sentry on duty interrupted. *Shh, silence. You are not allowed to talk here.*

It had been some time since Hamir had met anyone other

than Pakistanis. Though he wasn't allowed to converse, the mere presence of Asif was comforting. He was also happy that Asif had survived the battle.

After a few minutes the catering assistant entered the room carrying the breakfast tray and its delicious aroma filled the room. Hamir was famished.

The nurse noticed that the tray included eggs. Assuming Hamir was a vegetarian she ticked off the catering assistant.

'Why have you brought him eggs? Don't you know he's a Hindu? He won't eat eggs!'

'No madam, sahab eats eggs!' CHM Asif interjected. He knew his company commander well. Though a prisoner himself, his concern for his company commander drew a smile on Hamir's face. He was amused by the conversation.

'Major, would you like to have the eggs?' the nurse inquired.

'Sure. I wouldn't mind!' he replied.

Hamir was handed his breakfast tray and he began eating, careful not to drop its contents. Having only one working hand in itself was problematic but his blindfold multiplied the degree of difficulty many times over. He ate slowly. First the buttered toast. Next he picked up the enamel mug containing tea. Meanwhile the nurse had returned. She noticed that Hamir hadn't eaten the eggs yet.

'See, didn't I tell you he doesn't eat the eggs!'

'I didn't eat them because I can't peel the boiled eggs, nurse,' he lifted his bandaged right arm to emphasize his point.

'Oh...sorry,' she replied, embarrassed by her oversight. She peeled the boiled eggs for Hamir and handed him the plate containing them, much to Asif's delight.

'Thank you,' he acknowledged with a smile.

'OK, you better get cleaned up now,' she ordered. 'The doctors will be coming on their morning rounds soon.'

The nursing assistant and barber joined hands in tidying Hamir up. The barber focused on his job giving Hamir a shave while the nursing assistant used a damp towel to dry-clean him. As a result of their efforts, Hamir looked fresh and felt good. They finished just in time as the doctors walked in for their morning inspection soon thereafter.

'There's no need for the blindfold any more. Please remove it,' someone ordered.

To Hamir's relief his blindfold was removed and he had his first look at his room. It was a largish room and there were many other wounded soldiers inside. Lying on a bed to his right was CHM Asif, who smiled at Hamir when he found him looking in his direction. He seemed genuinely happy to see his company commander.

'Good morning, Major,' one of the doctors said loudly, drawing Hamir's attention.

'Good morning, doctor,' Hamir replied, not sure of his rank as he was wearing a doctor's white jacket over his uniform. He studied Hamir's medical documents and inquired about his well-being. He then scribbled something in his notebook.

'Your wounds appear to be healing well. Your bones will set on their own but your wrist drop and the damaged nerve in your right hand require an operation. However, that will need to wait until the bullet wounds are fully healed.'

Hamir nodded. Then looking towards the nursing assistant the doctor said, 'Please give the officer a room for himself. He needs some privacy.'

The nursing assistant nodded in acknowledgment.

The doctor then put away his notebook—'OK, that's all. We will see you later, Major. Bye for now.'

The doctor and his entourage left the room.

As soon as they had left Hamir was wheeled out as he was to have a room to himself. But before he left Hamir was able to have a brief conversation with Asif. Though injured, Asif seemed fine and in good spirits.

Hamir's new room was about ten feet by ten feet. There was a single door and a small window. Other than his bed the only other furniture in the room was a small stool which was placed next to the fireplace. After he was helped into the bed a sentry entered the room and sat down on the stool.

'OK, sahab, you can rest now. No one will disturb you till lunch.' But Hamir felt the urge to relieve himself before he rested.

'Theek hai, par pehle mujhe toilet jana hai,' Hamir mentioned. *OK, but before that I need to use the toilet.*

'Uski zaroorat nahin hai, sahab, toilet yahan aa jayega,' the sentry replied, smiling. *You don't need to, sir. The toilet will come to you.*

'Nahin, nahin! Main theek hoon, apne aap chala jaunga!' Hamir exclaimed. *No, no! There's no need for that. I am fine, I can walk on my own!*

'Aap shayad mujhe samajh nahin paa rahe ho, sahab. Aap ek minute intezar kijiye, main abhi aata hoon,' he said. *I don't think you understand, sir. Excuse me for a minute, I will be right back.*

The sentry left and returned with the sanitation assistant carrying a bedpan in his hand. Hamir now understood what the doctor had meant when he had asked for privacy for him, and he was absolutely right. He definitely required privacy! Thankfully he now had the room to himself.

But the thought that he would be doing everything, including his daily ablutions, within the confines of his room was a terrible nightmare. To make matters worse he had no idea how long he would remain a prisoner; after all the war was only two weeks old.

What Hamir didn't know was that it was the sixteenth of December, and a ceasefire had been declared, signalling the end of the war.

Alwar, India

The morning puja had just been completed.

Laxmi's father, 'Kanwarsa' as he was addressed by all his children, as well as his grandchildren, was a hardworking police officer. A religious man, he would gather his family in prayer every morning before he left for office. At about seven the entire family would sit down on the floor on a large cotton mattress. Prayers were said loudly accompanied by the beats of a dholak and the clanging of small brass cymbals. The prayers would normally take an hour.

The Road to Recovery

Kanwarsa, Shri Jodh Singh ji, IPS and his wife. Laxmi's parents.

Now that the prayers had been said a round of tea was being served while the family engaged in some informal chatter. The telephone rang abruptly, interrupting the conversation. A call so early in the day was unusual especially as his office staff and friends were aware of his morning regime.

Kanwarsa walked up to the phone. The entire family watched him in rapt attention as he picked up the receiver. There was a short conversation at the end of which his face turned pale. Bausa, Laxmi's mother, who immediately noticed his facial expression, was the first one to speak. Conversations at home were generally in Rajasthani.

'Kain huyo,' she asked. *What happened?* Kanwarsa didn't reply, choosing to remain silent.

'Kun ho?' she tried again. *Who was it?*

'Jawaisa ki paltan unh phone ho,' he finally replied. *It was a phone from our son-in-law's battalion.*

'Kain bolya wey?' Laxmi was anxious. *What did they say?*

'They said they could not find him. He's been declared missing!'

Laxmi fainted right where she had been seated. Her mother rushed to get a glass of water. Vikram clung to his mother, worried, while Vijay stood over her looking rather confused.

Bausa sprinkled some water on Laxmi's face and she opened her eyes. For a moment she seemed fine but the moment she saw Vijay's face she burst out crying. Both boys had no idea what was happening, but seeing their mother distraught began crying as well. Bausa's attempts to calm them all down were in vain. Kanwarsa walked up to Laxmi.

'Bai, eenya kyun kare hai?' he said, patting Laxmi on her head. *Why are you behaving like this?* Laxmi said nothing. She seemed dazed and speechless.

Bausa lifted Vijay up and took him to her room. She unlocked her steel cupboard and from her secret trove drew out a fistful of cashew nuts and handed them to him. Vijay, suitably distracted, stopped crying and ran away outside with his goodies. But Vikram wouldn't leave his mother's side and clung to her.

Kanwarsa spoke to his daughter again trying his best to console her. 'If they can't find him, it doesn't mean something bad has happened to him. He is fine, I am telling you!' he said.

On hearing her father's words Laxmi seemed better. Kanwarsa's words always had a calming effect.

A religious man, Kanwarsa was universally respected. His words had authority and a finality about them. If he said Hamir was fine, it meant he was fine! At least that was what the family believed.

Laxmi gathered herself, got up and left for her room. In a few minutes she was back to her daily chores and she went about her business in silence and in a mechanical fashion. It was hard for her to concentrate.

Meanwhile the nation was in a different mood altogether. Pakistan's surrender had just been announced and people broke out in jubilation. Alwar celebrated too. The sound of crackers rent the air. Sweets were distributed.

The Road to Recovery

There was no celebration, however, in her father's house. The topic of war was now taboo and no one wished to broach it.

In the loneliness of night while the household slept, Laxmi tossed and turned in her bed besieged with worry about her future. What would happen to her and her children if Hamir didn't return? How would she raise them without a father, she thought.

She couldn't sleep and there was no use remaining in bed. She got up and walked out to the garden. It was a cold night but being outdoors somehow made her feel better. She was beset with negative thoughts that were hard to shrug off. *Am I destined to become a widow?* she wondered.

Only twenty-five, she was young and had a long life ahead. She had seen how widows were treated in her village: relegated to dark corners of the house, considered inauspicious. They lived sad, pathetic lives. Dressing up, wearing bright, happy colours or ornaments of any kind was forbidden. They were not allowed to join any festivity or celebration. They were expected to grieve for their husbands till the end of their lives.

The thought of her donning white clothes throughout her life horrified her. She returned to her room, dragged her suitcase from under her bed and ran her hands through her clothes, some of which she had so enthusiastically purchased only recently, during her holiday in Europe.

She cried silently, holding her lovely clothes. *Will I ever get to wear these clothes? Am I to remain draped in inauspicious whites forever? This can't be happening to me. Kanwarsa said all will be fine!*

Her father's words were all she had for comfort that night and it was quite a while before she returned to her bed.

Military Hospital, Pakistan

Hamir had spent a few days alone in his room when one afternoon he found the staff making preparations for an incoming patient. It was obvious that Hamir would soon have company and he was curious to see who it would be.

In the evening a patient was brought in. After ensuring that the patient was settled in the medical staff left the room, leaving them both alone. Hamir remained silent, waiting for the sentry to leave the room, which he did later in the afternoon. Hamir walked up to the new patient and introduced himself.

'Hello, I am Major Hamir Singh,' he said.

'Good evening, sir, I am Second Lieutenant Ganga Ram Chaudhary, 3/9 GR, sir.'

The officer looked young, not more than twenty-five years old. He was tall and slim. He had bandages on his face and the back of his head.

'OK, how are you?' Hamir asked.

'I am fine, sir, just some minor injuries,' he replied.

'What happened? How did you land up here?'

'Oh, sir, just some bad luck. Our battalion was carrying out an attack from the Pathankot Sector, close to Shakargarh. We were to capture Chatrana, a village on the outskirts of Shakargarh. I was part of the leading platoon for the attack across the River Bein.'[15]

'That must have been a challenge; it gets pretty cold in those areas,' Hamir interjected.

'Yes, sir, it was. We waded across the river despite its freezing water. We were lucky. There was hardly any opposition and we were able to capture the objective.'

'Great, then what happened?'

'Counterattack, sir! Tanks, mortars, artillery. My platoon faced the brunt of the attack. We kept waiting for reinforcements, but they never seemed to arrive,' he lamented.

'Why, where was the remaining battalion?' Hamir asked.

'That's the problem, sir. Due to the heavy enemy onslaught the remaining battalion was stuck on the home side of the river, while we waited on the other side,' Chaudhary explained.

'OK, I got it. So you were cut off from your battalion. So even if your battalion withdrew, you wouldn't have been able to get back!' Hamir remarked.

'Precisely, sir. We fought from where we were and held on

to our position until the enemy's large numbers overwhelmed us. I lost many men, either killed or captured. I was wounded too and lost consciousness.'

The action Second Lieutenant Chaudhary described seemed very similar to his own. 'And what about your Company Commander, what happened to him?' Hamir inquired.

'No idea, sir. I know that he was injured, I only hope he survived. My boys fought really well that day, sir, really proud of them,' he replied.

'I am sure they did,' Hamir commented.

The young second lieutenant seemed a bit disturbed. He was silent for some time. Hamir allowed him time to regain his composure until he spoke again.

'Sir, when I gained consciousness, I found myself being dumped into a truck along with some of my men. We were kicked, slapped and subjected to the choicest of verbal abuses,' Chaudhary said.

'I can understand. You must have given them a bloody nose, they would have obviously been livid!'

'Yes, sir, and they didn't seem to want any prisoners. After driving us for about thirty minutes, we were ordered to dismount and line up against a wall… We were fired upon, sir. One of the enemy soldiers emptied his entire magazine on us. Many were injured and fell to the ground,' Chaudhary explained.

'Oh! So that's how you got injured!'

'No, sir, I was lucky. I remained unhurt. They then decided to take me alive and interrogate me. The third-degree torture during the interrogation is the cause of these injuries to me, sir.'

'But what information were they expecting to get from you? After all you are only a youngster and would know nothing,' Hamir commented.

'Absolutely, sir! Thankfully they realized this soon enough and the torture stopped. My wounds were turning septic and so—here I am!' Chaudhary smiled.

Hamir looked at the young officer with respect. Lieutenant Chaudhary had been through hell. 'That's quite an experience for a young officer. You sure have come a long way,' Hamir remarked. Chaudhary continued smiling nonchalantly.

For Hamir, Lieutenant Chaudhary's company was a welcome and positive development. It was nice to have someone to talk to without being guarded. He enjoyed the opportunity and they continued conversing.

'Tell me about yourself, Lieutenant. Where are you from?'

'Sir, I belong to Jodhpur.[16] My father is a farmer and we are a large family,' Chaudhary told him.

'Oh! So how's the farm doing?' Hamir asked.

'Not too well, sir. After a couple of years of severe famine… life had been pretty tough for my father. As I mentioned, he has a large family to support.'

'Yes, I understand, Ganga. A farmer's life is tough,' Hamir commented.

'Correct, sir. You know, I had always nursed an ambition to become a doctor. But seeing my father's predicament I felt I needed to help him by supplementing his income.'

'Good of you!'

'I enlisted for the Indian Navy. During my training I appeared and cleared both the entrance exam and interview of the Officers Training School at Madras. I joined 3/9 only in August this year.'

'Remarkable, what a journey! Vizag–Madras–Pathankot and now here!'

'Yes, sir. Quite a journey!' he smiled.

They spent the better part of the evening chatting up. The sentry on duty was kind enough to allow their conversation. Since they switched to Hindi from time to time their conversation provided the sentry some means of entertainment. Both Hamir and Chaudhary belonged to Rajasthan and they had many common topics to discuss. Their conversation continued until late at night when, exhausted, they finally fell asleep.

By the time Hamir woke up the next day Lieutenant Chaudhary had been taken away. Hamir would miss having company and wondered whether he would ever get to see young Ganga Ram Chaudhary again.

January 1972. Alwar

As always Vijay ate slowly. If he didn't hurry up he'd be late for school. Laxmi had no option but to go in for her time-tested technique. A poor eater that Vijay was, Laxmi had mastered a number of techniques to coax him to finish his food. Today it was time for the tick mark technique, which was among Vijay's favourites. Laxmi would allow him to draw a tick mark in his book every time he ate a spoonful of his porridge. Vijay had soon gained momentum ticking away, chuckling loudly with each tick, when the doorbell rang. *Had the school bus arrived?* Laxmi wondered.

'It's for you, jija, there's a soldier outside,' Padam, Laxmi's younger brother, informed her.

'Mere liye?' Laxmi sounded surprised. *For me? Why would a soldier come all the way to Alwar to meet me?* Puzzled, she rushed outside to find a soldier in the Grenadiers uniform waiting for her.

'Ram Ram, memsahab! Main Hamir sahab ka samaan laya hoon,' he said. *Good morning, ma'am. I have brought Hamir sahab's belongings.* He went to the cycle rickshaw waiting outside and returned with a large suitcase and a holdall. Laxmi recognized the suitcase immediately. It was a dark tan leather suitcase which they had bought together, just prior to leaving Nigeria.

'Kya sahab bhi aa rahe hain?' *Is sahab also returning?*

'Yeh to mujhe pata nahin, memsahab. Mujhe toh sirf samaan wapas karne ka hukam mila tha,' he replied. *I don't know, ma'am. I was only asked to return the luggage.*

Alarmed, she disappeared into the house, tears streaming down her face. One look at Laxmi's ashen face and Kanwarsa realized that something was amiss.

'What happened, bai, why are you crying?' he said.

'A soldier has come back to return his[17] belongings. Why has the soldier brought them back? Has something happened to him?' Laxmi blurted out.

'Bai, nothing has happened to Jawaisa. He's fine! Just trust me. He will be back,' Kanwarsa replied, calmly.

He walked up to the door, greeted the soldier and invited him in. A cup of tea was ordered for the soldier while Hamir's luggage was placed in Laxmi's room. Laxmi stood near the door listening to their conversation.

The soldier informed Kanwarsa that as per military procedure the belongings of soldiers missing in action are required to be returned to the family. Accordingly he had been sent to deliver the luggage.

Nothing had been heard about Hamir since the afternoon of 14 December. The unit feared the worst. The men who returned from battle had last seen a badly injured Hamir engaged in a hand-to-hand fight with the Pakistanis.

Since there had been no news about him for almost a month, most in the battalion believed that Hamir had been martyred too, like the other three company commanders. While he had come to return Hamir's belongings he hoped that Hamir would return one day.

Kanwarsa thanked the soldier and saw him off.

Laxmi, who had been listening, was distraught and burst into tears when she saw her father return after seeing the soldier off. Kanwarsa calmly consoled Laxmi.

'Bai, I have told you so many times. Nothing will happen to Jawaisa. Don't you believe me?' he said.

'I do, but I heard what the soldier said!' Laxmi replied, sobbing.

'But you haven't heard what Maharaj said when I spoke to him. He has assured me that Jawaisa will return. There is nothing to worry!' Kanwarsa assured Laxmi. 'And please be strong. What will the children think?' he added.

Kanwarsa's spiritual guru, referred to as 'Maharaj', was a revered man and every member of Kanwarsa's large family had implicit faith in him. Maharaj was himself based in Lucknow but his presence in the house was ensured by means of a photo of him in meditation. The photo was omnipresent in the house, allowing everyone the opportunity to seek his blessings.

Hearing her father's words made Laxmi feel better. She wiped away her tears, walked up to the photo of Maharaj, folded her hands in reverence and looked up at him. *Thank you, Maharaj. My husband will be back. I will never doubt it again*, she promised.

Military Hospital, Pakistan

As days passed Hamir was beset with loneliness. He missed having someone to talk to and it had been quite a while since they had taken away Lieutenant Chaudhary, the last person he had for company. His loneliness was compounded by the fact that he was lodged at the hospital's isolation ward, the section where soldiers with infectious diseases were kept segregated.

Designed for isolation the location was itself at one end of the hospital, where activity was severely restricted. His ten foot by ten foot room, primarily meant for JCOs, worsened his sense of isolation. His only company was the lone sentry who sat on the small wooden stool inside the already cramped room. He hardly got to see the other sentry who stood outside, unless he entered the room to chase away an unwanted visitor.

The sentries were generally benign looking senior citizens. They were mostly retired soldiers recalled for certain duties on commencement of the war. Each sentry had a two-hour tour of duty. When the guard changeover took place Hamir would sometimes overhear their handing/taking over instructions.

'Don't you dare go to sleep and don't ever forget that he's a commando. He may seem helpless, but if you doze off—then God help you! He will kill you and escape. Always remain alert!'

They were extremely wary of commandos and given that they were certain Hamir was a commando they would never take chances. As a result the sentries kept an extremely close and uncomfortable watch on him.

His main conversational partners were also the very same sentries. However, their conversation was dependent on two factors—their mood and the time of day. Since guards were forbidden from conversing with the prisoners they would avoid interacting with Hamir during the day. Their conversations would be restricted to late in the night, after the penultimate visit of the day by the nursing assistant.

A combination of lack of physical exercise and frequent naps during the day would sometimes make it difficult for Hamir to sleep at night. On such occasions he would toss and turn in his bed, struggling to sleep. If there was a friendly soldier on duty he would notice and engage him in conversation, secure in the knowledge that they were alone.

The responsibility of looking after Hamir was turned over every week between various regiments of the Pakistani army. Among these Hamir's favourites were the soldiers of the Frontier Force Regiment whose friendly Pathans made life in the hospital bearable.

The Pathans, tough soldiers during their younger days, had mellowed down with age. They were simple souls and would converse easily. Most of them had very fond memories of their life in the pre-Partition Indian Army.

'Those were the days, sir. I served in Hyderabad and Calcutta. It used to take us eight to ten days to reach home on leave. What fun we had! We used to eat together, play together. We would even celebrate festivals together—Holi, Diwali, Eid, you name it,' they would reminisce.

They lamented the fact that India had been partitioned and loathed politicians who they blamed for the Partition and the wars since. They were always respectful, relaxed and would happily allow Hamir some concessions, not overtly perturbed by regulations. At night the sentry in the room would even leave Hamir alone and would join the other sentry outside.

'Sahab, just relax and go to sleep. Our changing of duties will disturb you at night. I am sitting outside if you need me, just call out.' This became the informal arrangement whenever the Frontier Force soldiers were on duty.

On the other hand soldiers of Punjabi origin had an entirely different attitude. They were strict, officious and would rarely engage in conversation. When it was their tour of duty the nights would be especially boring for Hamir as he would have to spend his time alone with no scope for any conversation whatsoever.

His day would begin at six every morning. The nurse on duty would come to check up on him and administer his medicine. Thereafter she would return after lunch and her final visit would be at six in the evening. Since his hand was in a plaster and required no further treatment for at least six weeks Hamir was spared the daily visit of a doctor. In any case he suffered from no other medical ailments.

The nursing assistant on night duty was usually a young Bengali man—Havildar Choudhury. He belonged to a village near Dhaka, East Pakistan. A pleasant man, he was well educated. He would check on Hamir after dinner and would often linger on to converse with him. Their conversation was generally in English. The sentry therefore had no idea what they were talking about, although Havildar Choudhury would avoid controversial topics. He would chat about his family and share anecdotes about his life in East Pakistan. Hamir enjoyed his company and looked forward to their conversations.

Food was wholesome and satisfactory. Breakfast was invariably continental consisting of eggs, bread, porridge and a cup of tea. Lunch and dinner was generally local cuisine and chicken biryani was served frequently. Initially the mess staff was doubtful if Hamir would eat the non-vegetarian dishes as the meat being served to them was halal. However, they soon realized that Hamir had no such inhibitions; he was after all the company commander of Muslim troops.

His life, though comfortable, was boring due to his loneliness. There would be times when other than the nursing assistant, who would himself be absent quite often, there would be no one to speak to for days at a stretch. To make matters worse he was not provided with any newspapers, television or radio. He lost count of days, dates and very often couldn't tell the time of day; his brand new Seiko watch had been confiscated. His main sources of information were his brief chats with the sentries or the Bengali nursing assistant.

Almost as a daily ritual there would be a large number of inquisitive people peering through the only window in Hamir's room to catch a glimpse of the 'Hindu' soldier. He felt like a caged animal in a zoo and initially it upset him. He soon got used to it as he realized it was just the harmless inquisitiveness of the locals for whom seeing a Hindu soldier was a novelty, like the two ladies who had offered him 'keenu'. Besides, their interest had also been sparked by the story of his valour despite being badly injured. The fact that he was supposedly a commando added to his aura.

One day Havildar Choudhury entered the room looking a little tense. He wasn't his normal self.

'Sir, this is my last day at this hospital,' Choudhury remarked.

'Oh! So you have been posted out, is it? Where are you going?' Hamir inquired.

'Actually, sir, I am going home to East Pakistan, or should I say Bangladesh. The war ended a few days back and East Pakistan is now Bangladesh. All Bengalis are being rounded up here in Pakistan. I don't know what will happen now but I am hoping that they will relocate us to Bangladesh,' he explained.

Hamir was slightly taken aback. He hadn't realized that the war was over.

'When did the war end?' he asked.

'16 December was the ceasefire, sir,' replied Choudhury.

'Just imagine that! Two more days and I would have seen the end of the war. I wouldn't be here, and by the way, I don't even know where I am!' Hamir remarked, smiling.

Havildar Choudhury seemed surprised at Hamir's ignorance.

'Sir, you are in Command Military Hospital, that is CMH, Rawalpindi,' he said.

'Oh, I see. Rawalpindi! You know, Choudhury, I would never have known. I am really cut off here, with no company or access to newspapers or radio,' Hamir lamented.

'I agree with you, sir. I don't understand why you are being treated this way. In the other officers' ward there are fifteen Indian officers. Not only do they have the company of each other they are also provided newspapers and even have a television. You are the only Indian officer being meted out this special treatment,' Choudhury added.

The Road to Recovery

'And God knows why!' Hamir interjected.

'I'm sorry, sir, there is nothing I can do in this regard. I only hope you get better treatment in the future. As for me I don't think I will get the opportunity to meet you again. I wish you a speedy recovery and the very best. Your hand will be fine soon and inshallah we shall meet again in better times. Farewell, sir. It was nice interacting with you.'

'Farewell, Havildar Choudhury. Thank you for looking after me and keeping me company. I wish you and your new country the very best. May peace be with you and your family.'

The nursing assistant's words remained in Hamir's mind for a considerable period of time. He was intrigued as to why he was being given this special treatment and being kept away from the other Indian officers. He decided that the next day he would demand newspapers. It was time he spoke up.

One disturbing thought kept playing in his mind. As of now only two Indians knew of his being alive. Second Lieutenant Ganga Ram Chaudhary and CHM Asif. *What if Second Lieutenant Chaudhary, Asif and I were never sent back to India or, even worse, eliminated at some juncture?* It was widely believed that many POWs of the 1965 Indo-Pakistan war and the 1962 Sino-Indian war had not returned home. *Was that the real purpose of keeping me away from other Indian prisoners?* These disturbing thoughts troubled him for some time. He felt helpless, worried and sad.

~

The next morning Hamir had to be woken up. Normally he would be wide awake by the time the nursing assistant arrived at six. But plagued as he was by negative thoughts at dinner the previous night he had had trouble sleeping. By the time he finally slept it was close to dawn.

'Wake up, sir. You are still sleeping?' It was the morning nurse in her usual morning cheer. Hamir just grunted in acknowledgment.

'Get up, sir, have your tea!' she requested politely while handing him his morning quota of tablets.

As Hamir sipped his tea his gaze fell upon the sentry seated next to him. He was not the person who had been on duty the previous night. He was much older and had a long grey beard. The sentry's eyes were fixed on Hamir's face making him a little uncomfortable.

Hamir was curious to know what had happened to the previous sentry. He looked towards the new sentry and said, 'And who are you soldier? I thought someone else was on duty last night.'

'You are right, sir. He fell suddenly ill, early this morning. I, ex-Havildar Major[18] Jalaluddin[19] have replaced him,' the new sentry spoke softly and with respect.

'OK. I see, Major,' Hamir nodded. Havildar majors were colloquially referred to as Major. Hamir spoke to Jalaluddin with the respect he deserved; he was, perhaps, as old as his father.

Meanwhile the nurse walked up to Hamir and said, 'Sir, I see you lying down the whole time. This is not good. I have a suggestion.'

'And what's that, sister?' Hamir asked, curious.

'You need to move around a bit,' she suggested.

'Move around! Even if I shift my position on my bed suddenly these guards are on my case. They wouldn't let me move, even a bit,' Hamir replied.

'Don't worry, sir, I will tell the sentry and the security officer,' she said. 'Now please get up.' She helped Hamir onto his feet and watched as he gingerly took a few steps.

'That's it, sir. Please make it a point to walk for at least thirty minutes every day, even if it means walking within the four walls of this room,' she said.

'Thank you, sister, I will. But I have one request too.'

'Sure, sir. What is it?' she asked.

'Sister, please give me some newspapers to read. It's so boring for me to remain cooped up here with no one to talk to and nothing to read!'

'I understand, sir. But this is beyond me. I suggest you make that request to the Commandant during his inspection,' the nurse replied.

'God knows when he'll come here next,' Hamir said, irritated.

'Sir, you know he makes his rounds every Monday morning. It's only three days away. Be patient for a few more days. I feel your request is reasonable. You must make it to the Commandant,' she suggested.

'Fine! I think that's what I will do. Thank you,' Hamir replied.

The nurse left the room. Jalaluddin had been keenly listening to the conversation between Hamir and the nurse. 'You don't get newspapers, sir?' he asked.

'No, Major. That's the problem. They don't understand how difficult it is to pass my time here. It's hard, really.'

'No problem, sir. I am on duty tonight and I will get you a newspaper,' Jalaluddin promised.

Hamir was pleasantly surprised by the attitude of his new sentry. For some reason he seemed to have taken a liking to Hamir.

In the evening when the guards changed Hamir was happy to see Jalaluddin return. Whether he had brought a newspaper or not Hamir couldn't make out. He wouldn't ask him either as he didn't want to embarrass the genial old man should he have forgotten their last conversation. In any case it was too early in the night for him to read the forbidden newspaper and someone could inadvertently let out their secret. That would jeopardize the position of the old man. It was not worth the risk.

Hamir washed up, had his dinner and lay down. The nursing assistant arrived at ten for his final round. They exchanged pleasantries and chatted for a while until he departed, leaving Hamir alone with Jalaluddin for the night. The old man sensed Hamir's expectation by the look on his face.

'Don't worry, sir, I have got the newspaper,' he blurted out. He had kept it inside too long. He thrust his hand inside his shirt and took out a folded newspaper.

'Here, sahabji,' he said, handing Hamir the newspaper.

Hamir began unfolding it at once with Jalaluddin watching,

satisfied that he had been of help. When Hamir's eyes fell on the paper he realized that he couldn't read a word! The paper was in Urdu. Hamir, though disappointed, didn't allow his feelings to show. He continued scanning the paper, glancing through the photos and advertisements. Despite his best efforts he couldn't keep up the charade beyond about ten minutes.

He folded the paper and handed it back to Jalaluddin. 'Thank you, I have read it,' Hamir said.

'So fast? How is that possible?'

Hamir just didn't have the heart to lie to him any more. 'Major, it's an Urdu paper,' Hamir remarked.

'Yes, so what?'

'I don't know Urdu,' Hamir explained.

'What! Then how did you become an officer?' he exclaimed, surprised. The old man could not believe that one could become an officer without knowing Urdu.

Hamir smiled politely. He had no explanation for his 'ignorance'. While it was true that in pre-Partition India a large number of people studied Urdu, as far as Hamir was concerned he had not learned the language. Jalaluddin seemed a bit disappointed, but not for long.

'Koi baat nahin, sahabji. Duniya ki khabrein main hi aapko bata doonga,' he said politely. *Doesn't matter, sir. I will give you the latest in the world myself.* True to his word Jalaluddin shared what little news of the world he could rattle off at the spur of the moment to Hamir's amusement.

After he had finished Hamir thanked Jalaluddin, who brushed the thanks aside and said, 'Sir, when I served in the army I had many Hindu friends like you. We served together, lived together and even died together. We would share everything, festivals, food, laughter, everything. My heart pains to see you like this!'

'I agree with you, Major. My father served in the World War with many colleagues like yourself. Many of his friends are in Pakistan today,' Hamir replied.

'Achha, aapke waalid bhi fauj mein the? Jaisa baap, waisa beta! Kitni achhi baat hai,' Jalaluddin remarked. *Oh, your father was in the army too? Like father, like son! How nice.*

'Haan, Major. Hindi mein ek kahawat hai: "Sapere ka beta sapera hi hota hai!"' Hamir added. *A snake charmer's son is always a snake charmer!*

Both of them broke into hearty laughter and their conversation continued. They talked late into the night until Jalaluddin turned emotional and requested to be excused.

'Ya Allah! Why did I live to see this day? I will not volunteer for this duty again. I can't take it,' he confessed. 'Dil dukhta hai, janab!' *My heart aches in sadness, sir.*

Hamir could sense the old man's emotion and he was touched too. It was a poignant moment. An ode perhaps to the comradeship that soldiers of both countries enjoyed till only a few decades ago.

'Good night, Major, it was a pleasure meeting you,' Hamir remarked as he retired for the night. Either due to his age or perhaps his request not to be assigned on sentry duty at CMH, Rawalpindi, Hamir never met Jalaluddin again.

Although it was late Hamir couldn't sleep for some reason. His thoughts went back to the time when he had been referred to as a 'sapere ka beta' (snake charmer's son) during an NCC camp, which Hamir was attending as a young NCC Cadet in the summer of 1955.

June 1955. Delhi Cantonment, Field Firing Ranges

Hamir was excited as the camp was about to begin. He had worked very hard while training with the Artillery Battalion of the National Cadet Corps (NCC). Now it was time to put to practical use what they had so far learnt only in theory. As a part of the camp the cadets would be visiting an artillery regiment while it was carrying out its field firing at the Vasant Ranges, south of Delhi, where the present-day Vasant Range Colony (Shankar Vihar) is located.

Field artillery has three distinct parts: the forward observer (or FO), the fire direction centre (FDC) and the actual guns themselves.

The forward observer observes the target using his binoculars and controls fire of the guns using his radio. The FO is therefore located at an observation point from where he can observe the artillery shells as they fall. From here he passes corrections to the FDC to ensure that future rounds fall at the target.

The FO communicates directly with the battery FDC, of which there is normally one per battery of four to eight guns.

The battery FDC computes firing data—ammunition to be used, powder charge, fuse settings, the direction to the target, the quadrant elevation to be fired at to reach the target and the number of rounds to be fired on the target by each gun. Though it is largely automated today the computation of data was a manual process of mathematical calculation in the earlier days. Once calculated this data is relayed via radio or wire communications to the gun crews who would use the data while laying the guns.

The guns are the third part—gun crews point the guns in the proper direction, elevate or drop them as required, and fire rounds based on the orders from the FDC.

The young NCC cadets were to be given a feel of the activities carried out at the gun end. They would witness the gun drills and carry out the technical calculations along with the personnel at the FDC.

Since Hamir was a science student getting a hang of the mathematical calculations at the FDC wasn't too difficult. After just a couple of shoots where his calculations proved absolutely accurate he had managed to catch the attention of Major Shiv Singh, the battery commander. An impressed Shiv Singh walked up to the commanding officer of the NCC Battalion and said, 'Sir, there's a cadet who has done extremely well at the gun end. You must meet him.'

'Is that so? Please send him to me,' the CO, Colonel Bhag Singh replied. Young Hamir was presented before him.

'So, son, I believe you have done very well. Will you be able to direct a shoot from the target end?' Bhag Singh asked him.

*Young Hamir with fellow cadets at NCC camp in Delhi.
His face is not visible in the photograph.*

'Sure, sir. If I get an opportunity,' Hamir replied.

'OK, I will give you one chance. Let's see how good you really are!' Hamir was dispatched to the observation point from where he would direct the shoot.

Whether it was beginner's luck or his practical common sense, one couldn't say, but Hamir was able to get the rounds on the target after just a few corrections. For a novice his performance was exceptional.

Bhag Singh was astonished. 'Well done, son. You have done very well. Are you keen to join the army?'

'Yes, sir, definitely,' Hamir replied.

'OK, tell me your father's name?' he remarked. 'I will advise him on how to go about the process.'

'Colonel Kalyan Singh, sir.'

'Colonel Kalyan Singh of 2 Field Regiment?' Bhag Singh questioned. He seemed surprised.

'41 Field Regiment,' Hamir corrected him.

'Arre, originally 2 Field Regiment, I know him son!' he

interjected. He was right. Colonel Kalyan Singh belonged to 2 Field Regiment. But he had raised the 41 Field Regiment at Jhansi, so technically he now belonged to 41 Field Regiment. 'Why didn't you tell me that before?'

Meanwhile, Major Shiv Singh, who had been conducting the firing, joined them. 'This boy is unbelievable, sir. What a shoot! I don't know how he did it!' he exclaimed.

'Shiv Singh, always remember, sapere ka beta sapera hi hota hai!' Bhag Singh remarked. 'This young man is the son of the renowned gunner Colonel Kalyan Singh.'

Hamir smiled shyly as they broke out laughing.

Command Military Hospital, Rawalpindi

Hamir often thought about Laxmi and his family back home. He wondered whether they knew where he was and what had happened to him. It had been a month and a half since his capture. Surely they would have got the news.

But the reality was that back in India Hamir was still listed as missing in action. No one knew where he was or whether he was even alive.

As a part of his duties the subedar major of the hospital would visit all the wards regularly to inquire about the food and well-being of the patients. During his rounds he would always make it a point to converse with Hamir for some time. The SM was always respectful and courteous. He seemed genuinely concerned about Hamir's well-being.

One evening, after the usual queries the subedar major casually remarked, 'Sahab, hamare ek bade officer aapko jante hain. Aapke bare mein poochte rehte hain,' he said. *Sahab, one of our very senior officers knows you. He keeps asking about you from time to time.*

Hamir was puzzled. The only officers he had met since his capture were majors, except of course the commandant of the hospital who was a colonel. The commandant didn't need to ask about his well-being, he could meet Hamir any time. As it is he met him every Monday morning during his weekly inspections.

'Kaun hain, sahab, yeh "bade" officer?' Hamir queried. *Who is this very senior officer?* The subedar just ignored the question, acting as if he hadn't heard it at all.

'OK, sahab, I need to leave, I have work to do. Khuda hafiz.'

The subedar major's innocuous statement had Hamir thinking for some time. He tried to recollect the sequence of events since his capture. It didn't help, he still couldn't figure out who in Pakistan could be interested in his well-being.

His curiosity having been triggered Hamir tried even harder. He now went further back in time—to November 1969.

November 1969. Nigerian Defence Academy, Kaduna, Nigeria

Hamir had settled into his assignment as an instructor in the Nigerian Defence Academy at Kaduna, Nigeria. He really enjoyed his job as it provided him professional satisfaction as well as met his personal requirements.

Although primarily posted as a weapon instructor for the young cadets, Hamir was popular among them especially

Hamir as an instructor at the Nigerian National Defence Academy at Kaduna, Nigeria.

because of his sporting skills. It was not uncommon to find him playing football with his cadets or sparring with them in the boxing ring. The social life was enjoyable and Kaduna provided the family the opportunity to engage in their hobbies, and gave Hamir adequate time to be with them, which he greatly valued.

One day during his morning class Hamir developed a severe toothache. As the pain was unbearable he excused himself and made a beeline for the infirmary. The duty doctor immediately referred him to a civilian dentist who had been empanelled by the Nigerian Defence Academy to treat the foreign officers. At about ten o'clock he reported at the dentist's clinic in Kaduna city dressed in his military uniform.

After having parked his car he headed for the receptionist's counter armed with his referral. The receptionist requested Hamir to wait for some time as the dentist was busy with a dental procedure. Accordingly Hamir proceeded to the waiting room where he would await his turn.

While he waited Hamir happened to notice the dentist's credentials which had been proudly displayed on a notice board. The dentist was of Pakistani origin. This should be interesting, Hamir thought. He had never interacted with a Pakistani before. The traditional animosity and mistrust between Indians and Pakistanis was well known and here, in a few minutes, he was about to be treated by a Pakistani dentist!

After some time a distinguished looking, middle-aged man of Asian origin entered the room. He was smartly attired and from the manner in which the staff fussed around him it was evident that he was an important person. Hamir smiled at him and he nodded to acknowledge his presence.

'Good morning, Captain,' the man greeted Hamir as he sat down. Obviously the man had some knowledge of Indian Military uniform. *He must be an Indian*, Hamir thought. Though he couldn't recognize him. The man noticed that Hamir was struggling to place him.

'No we haven't met before, Captain. I am Adeeb Ali,'[20] he

remarked. The name still didn't ring a bell. 'So, how's life in NDA?' he continued.

Now Hamir was intrigued. *How does he know about NDA?*

'Good, sir! Can't complain!' he replied, a bit guarded.

'I have been there. It's a nice little place and you guys are doing a good job from what I hear from the Nigerians,' he continued.

Before he could reply the dentist made a sudden appearance, interrupting their conversation.

'Salaam alaikum, sir. I am sorry to keep you waiting! I wish you had just phoned me up before coming.'

'Alaikum salaam, doctor. I wish my tooth would have told me it would hurt!' he joked.

'Sorry to keep you waiting though,' the dentist said, laughing.

He then looked at Hamir. 'I hope you won't mind waiting for some more time, Captain? I need to attend to Brigadier Adeeb first. Have you met? He belongs to the Pakistan Army.'

Hamir nodded. 'No problem, doctor, please go ahead. Yes, we have just met,' he replied. Though it was the first time that he realized that Adeeb was a Pakistani brigadier.

'Thank you, Captain. I have seen your referral papers. It seems you have finally become wise!' he remarked, smiling. 'Your wisdom teeth have decided to show up. Unfortunately one of them has taken off in the wrong direction though. I am afraid that needs to be extracted; it's hurting the neighbouring tooth,' he added.

The dentist turned his attention to Adeeb.

'Sir, the treatment room will need to be sanitized. We just did a minor surgery. How about a cup of tea while we wait?' he suggested.

'Sure, why not? I suppose a hot liquid will ease my pain. But is having tea before treatment even permitted, doc?'

'Yes, sir, no problem at all,' he replied. 'Come, sir, let's go to my office. Captain, please allow me the pleasure of your company too,' he added.

He guided the two to his office and ordered a cup of tea.

Tea was served while the two conversed like old friends. So engrossed were they in their conversation that they almost forgot about Hamir's presence.

'Pardon us, Captain, we didn't mean to ignore you. You know we are good friends and we haven't met in a long time.'

'No problem, sir, I understand,' Hamir replied.

'Tell me, Captain Hamir, you don't mind being treated by a Pakistani dentist do you?' Brigadier Adeeb inquired, smiling.

'Not at all, sir. After all, we are professionals,' he replied.

'I like your answer, Captain,' the dentist commented.

'And I like you, Captain. You have spoken like a true soldier,' Brigadier Adeeb added. 'And we were part of the same country not very long ago.'

'Yes, sir. And incidentally I am a third-generation officer and many of the colleagues of my father and grandfather opted for Pakistan,' Hamir remarked. 'When we were part of the same army we fought together and now since Independence we have fought against each other in two wars like true professionals. I see no reason why we shouldn't respect each other's professionalism in a foreign country.'

'Absolutely! I entirely agree with you,' Adeeb remarked. 'See, doctor, I know a good guy when I see one.'

A technician entered the room and indicated that the treatment room was ready. 'I think we are ready for your treatment, sir, if you have had your tea.'

'Oh yes, I so enjoyed meeting this young man that I almost forgot the real purpose of my visit here!' Adeeb said.

'Then shall we?'

'Sure, but not before I shake the Captain's hand.' He walked towards Hamir and shook his hand firmly. 'It was a pleasure meeting you, young man. I shall never forget Captain Hamir Singh of the Indian Army. And if you ever happen to visit Pakistan, I promise to take good care of you.'

'It was nice meeting you too, sir. Thank you for your offer but I don't see myself visiting Pakistan in the near future,' Hamir laughed and the other two Pakistanis joined him, laughing loudly.

'And don't ever lose your wisdom, despite losing the wisdom tooth!' Adeeb joked, still laughing as he left the room.

The dentist was professional and competent. Hamir left the dental clinic after an hour relieved of his pain. It had been an interesting interaction with the Pakistanis.

~

Back to reality in Rawalpindi Hamir wondered whether the subedar major at CMH implied that the 'bade officer' was Brigadier Adeeb. After all, as far as Hamir was concerned, he was the only Pakistani senior officer he had ever known. It was possible that Adeeb had been promoted to the rank of major general and thus qualified to be considered a 'bade officer'.

However, even if it was indeed Adeeb, many questions remained in Hamir's mind. *How would Adeeb know that I am a prisoner of war? Was he the officer I met in the underground bunker near Daruchhian?* he wondered. Hamir would never get the answers to his questions. But as things turned out, whatever was happening right now was in Hamir's favour.

February 1972. Command Military Hospital, Rawalpindi

With the arrival of February the weather changed for the better. The nights were less severe and the mornings pleasant.

One day Hamir was woken up early in the morning by the barber, which was unusual. When Hamir looked around he noticed frenetic activity going on in his room. Housekeeping had been summoned and they were busy tidying things up. The room had been transformed into inspection order.

The nurse on duty made an unscheduled visit to ensure that Hamir was in a presentable condition. She had just about completed her inspection when the commandant entered the room. He was accompanied by a foreigner dressed in a suit with a prominent red cross affixed on the left pocket of his jacket.

'How are you doing, sir?' the foreigner inquired.

'I am fine, thank you,' Hamir replied.

'That's good. I am Walter Bremen[21] from the International Committee of the Red Cross, ICRC, and I'm here to note down your particulars,' the foreigner mentioned.

'Major, please feel free to share your particulars with him. As you know Pakistan always respects the Geneva Conventions,' the commandant interjected.

'Right, sir, I will do that,' Hamir said.

Mr Bremen now got down to the real purpose of his visit. He asked Hamir details such as his military identity number, unit and the area from where he had been captured. Thereafter he inquired about his family. While Hamir answered patiently, Bremen's assistant meticulously made notes in his diary. The commandant keenly followed the proceedings.

'I hope you're being treated well, Major?' Bremen inquired. 'The Pakistani military authorities have told us that they are giving you the best possible treatment.'

'Yes, I am being treated fine,' Hamir replied.

The commandant then went on to explain the nature of Hamir's injuries. He explained that further treatment was underway after which he would be repatriated. Bremen seemed satisfied.

'I'm sure you are receiving newspapers, magazines and books to read,' Bremen remarked.

Hamir looked towards the commandant who was nodding. But the question had been asked to Hamir and he wouldn't lie.

'No. At least not yet,' Hamir answered.

Mr Bremen glanced at the commandant in surprise. 'Colonel, may I request you to see to it that the officer gets something to read. It's absolutely essential for his mental rehabilitation.'

'Absolutely, Mr Bremen, there seems to have been some miscommunication. I will sort it out. He shall have them first thing tomorrow, for sure!' the commandant replied, a trifle embarrassed.

Hamir of course was delighted at the outcome of the conversation, but Bremen was not done yet. He took out a postcard from his briefcase and offered it to Hamir.

'Would you like to write a message to your family? I could have it sent.'

Hamir happily accepted the postcard. The small, light-brown, rectangular card had writing space adequate to pen down just about four to five lines.

Since Hamir's hand was in a cast he would need to write with his left hand. He penned down a few lines as neatly as he could.

He addressed Laxmi as Sapana so that she would understand that the card was really from her husband. He mentioned that he was fine although he had been wounded in his right hand. Since he was now writing with his left hand his handwriting may appear different and resemble Vijay's handwriting. Hamir was confident this would convince Laxmi that the letter was written by her husband should she be in doubt. He ended with his signature, or at least a signature as close to his that was possible with his left hand. After he had made use of all the space available on the card he handed over the postcard to Mr Bremen, who left shortly thereafter, wishing him the very best.

For Hamir it had been a momentous day and he was delighted with its outcome. Since the Pakistani authorities had allowed the ICRC representative to meet him it implied that they had decided to acknowledge that Hamir was in their custody and alive. His chances of being repatriated had increased manifold.

Once the ICRC shared their information with India Hamir's family would finally have credible news that he was alive and well. His postcard would be the icing on the cake.

As he lay down to sleep Hamir had much to thank the Almighty for. Or perhaps his anonymous benefactor—the 'bade officer'.

He slept well that night.

Alwar, Rajasthan

The children were excited as the festival of Holi was just two weeks away. Their preparations had begun in earnest commencing with the collection of empty eggs shells. They were an essential part of the Holi arsenal to be used as coloured-water-filled bombs.

In all such fun activities Laxmi was an eager participant. She would dexterously crack the egg shell while cooking eggs for breakfast, ensuring each child added at least two prospective bombs to his collection every day.

Having stockpiled a sizeable arsenal the kids were looking for an opportunity to test their weapons. Though Holi was still a few days away they had been waiting for an innocent target. The arrival of the postman proved to be just what they were waiting for.

The unsuspecting postman had no idea what hit him. He was wet and furious when he found two giggling kids scampering away on the roof of the house. But there was nothing he could do. He was at a senior police officer's residence and there was no point complaining. He rang the bell. A member of the staff opened the door and accepted the mail. Among the pile of letters lay an innocuous postcard. It was addressed to Laxmi. The staff member walked up to Laxmi's room and knocked on her door.

'Baisa, there's a postcard for you!'

Laxmi was a bit surprised. She couldn't recall when she had last received a card from someone. When she looked at the handwriting on the card she was further perplexed. It appeared to be written by a child. Gingerly, she read the contents of the card.

> *Dear Sapana,*
>
> *I know you will not recognize my handwriting. It's more like Vijay's. But that's because my right hand is injured and I am writing with my left hand. I am absolutely fine, I miss you all.*
>
> *Lovingly Yours,*
Hamir

Laxmi read the card a couple of times. She desperately wanted to believe it. No one but her husband addressed her as Sapana. She ran up to her mother to share the good news. Her mother was absolutely delighted and announced the news to all the others in the house while Laxmi headed to the temple to thank the Almighty. Her prayers had finally been answered.

A few days later the names of all the Indian prisoners in Pakistan were announced on All India Radio and published in the newspapers. Hamir's name was on that list, finally confirming that Hamir was alive and well.

Command Military Hospital, Rawalpindi

It was a Monday morning, which meant that the commandant of the hospital would be inspecting the wards. The inspection would normally commence with the officers' ward.

At nine-thirty the commandant arrived with a team of officers. There was a brief discussion between the medical specialist, surgical specialist and the commandant. After having a look at his papers and X-rays they concluded that it was time to remove Hamir's plaster. His hand had been in a cast for over six weeks and from the look of it the bones seemed to have healed.

'Major Hamir, it's time for you to say bye-bye to your plaster. Your hand looks fine. Let's remove it today, OK?' the commandant announced proudly.

Hamir's bones were badly damaged when he arrived at Rawalpindi. The complexity of the operation and the subsequent rehabilitation process had been a professional challenge for the hospital's doctors. Things seemed to have gone better than they expected. The commandant and his team of doctors were justified in taking pride in his recovery.

Hamir was happy too. It would be nice to get rid of the plaster. It would bring a degree of normality in his life.

At about eleven o'clock the nursing assistant reported to Hamir's room and escorted him to the surgical ward which was some distance away. The compounder who had been waiting for Hamir quickly cut through his plaster.

Free of the burden of the weight of plaster of Paris his hand felt extremely light. Except for the fact that it had turned pale and discoloured it seemed fine. However, he still couldn't keep his wrist upright.

'Now that your gunshot wounds and bones have healed the only issue left is your radial nerve. This would require another operation, only after that will you be able to control the movement of your wrist,' the surgical specialist remarked. 'This could be done in your country once you are repatriated or we could look at it at a later stage, if you are not repatriated in the near future.'

'Right, sir.'

'Well, there is not much more for me to do right now,' the doctor commented. 'I shall write my medical opinion for the future course of action.'

Hamir nodded, thanked the doctor and returned to his room. As he entered his room he found a small package lying on his bed. The package was addressed to him and had been delivered through the ICRC.

He had not yet got used to using his right hand. Due to its restricted mobility he had to grapple with the package for some time before he succeeded in opening the cardboard box.

Right on top of the contents was a long piece of olive green cloth. The moment he unfolded the cloth he realized that it was actually a turban. Below the cloth lay a neatly packed religious book in Gurmukhi script. *Why would someone send me a gift appropriate for a follower of the Sikh faith?* Hamir wondered. Then it struck him—his surname 'Singh' had once again been responsible for the confusion. This time it was the ICRC that had assumed he was a Sikh.

Hamir smiled. He was pretty sure that he could put the cloth to some use or the other. As for the religious book, he placed it inside the drawer of his bedside table and made a mental note to hand it over to a suitable person at an appropriate time.

Although the contents of the parcel were not of much use Hamir was grateful that someone had been thoughtful enough to think about the POWs. It felt nice to receive something from his motherland. It was also for the first time in his life that

Hamir had experienced the humanitarian work that the ICRC did and his respect for the organization grew tremendously.

~

A few days later Hamir found the barber making an excited entry into his room. Hamir could tell that he was dying to share some news.

'Sir, have you heard the good news?' he blurted out.

'No, what news?' Hamir replied.

'Last night Radio Pakistan announced that there is going to be an exchange of POWs between India and Pakistan. Some wounded prisoners would be returned to their countries tomorrow, 25 February,' he said, thrilled.

Hamir had been privy to such rumours. But an announcement to that effect on the radio definitely gave the rumours some credibility. If it did happen it would indeed be wonderful.

That evening a Pakistani officer reported at Hamir's bedside for paperwork in what appeared to be preparation for his repatriation. Although many of the staff came to bid him farewell Hamir wasn't too optimistic about his repatriation. For some inexplicable reason he was beset with negative thoughts.

The following day when the nurse arrived for her morning rounds she genuinely didn't expect to find him still there.

'You haven't changed your night dress—aren't you leaving today, sir?' she said, sounding surprised.

'No! I guess not. I am destined to spend more time in Pakistan! I am not being repatriated.'

'I wonder why, sir. Some officers and men are being repatriated!' she remarked. 'Why have you been ignored?'

Hamir had nothing to say. But he could sense the disappointment in her voice. Most of the hospital staff had become fond of their patient and had hoped the best for him. Hamir was disappointed too, his foreboding had been proven right.

He tried to analyse the reasons for missing out. The only reason he could think of was that there were many more severely injured Indian POWs than himself. Possibly their medical needs were more urgent and hence they had been accorded priority in repatriation, whereas he was left behind.

Consequent to the exchange of prisoners several wounded Pakistani soldiers, repatriated from India, were admitted at CMH, Rawalpindi. The next morning one of them entered his room. He introduced himself as Major Hameed.[22] He mentioned that he had been a POW at Jabalpur, India and had just dropped in to see how Indian POWs were being treated at the CMH.

'How has your stay been, sir?' Hameed inquired. 'I hope our guys are treating you well?'

'My stay has been fine. They are treating us well, I guess,' Hamir replied. Hameed glanced around the room, which was very basic and bare.

'I hope you are getting something to read.'

'Yes, I occasionally get an old copy of the *Reader's Digest* magazine.'

'What? That's it!' He seemed surprised. 'What about newspapers?'

'No, I am not so lucky. This is all I get!' He showed him a December 1966 edition of the *Reader's Digest*. The Pakistani wasn't impressed at all.

'What about TV?'

'No such luck!' Hamir smiled.

'That's not fair! We were given newspapers and magazines right from day one in captivity. We had a TV too. We watched Doordarshan every single day. It was our lifeline,' he remarked. 'I must report this to the authorities. This is ridiculous!'

They conversed for some more time until it was time for lunch and Hameed left the room.

It was evident from the conversation that Pakistani POWs in India were being treated well. Whether Major Hameed's feedback would make a difference only time would tell.

~

Whether it was as a result of Hameed's feedback or some other reason, in the evening, an elderly Pakistani major came to check in on Hamir. His shoulder titles indicated that he belonged to 12 Cavalry.[23] Hamir had never seen him before.

'Hello, Major Hamir, I need some time with you. I need to note down some details.'

He knows me already, Hamir thought. *Possibly another interrogator!* He had got used to such visits, which occurred periodically.

'Sure, sir,' Hamir replied, not that he had an option.

The Pakistani major then began asking him innocuous questions. Hamir was a bit surprised with the questions. He repeated questions whose answers the Pakistanis already knew. In fact the interrogation seemed a sham. The major seemed more concerned about Hamir's well-being than the questions he asked. This visit must serve a different purpose, Hamir wondered.

After about ten to fifteen minutes the major got up, ready to leave.

'So how was your Rangers Course abroad, Commando? Your men say you did extremely well,' he asked.

'Good, sir, very educative but tough,' Hamir lied. He had never done the course. *Let them keep guessing*, he thought.

'OK, I think you must be tired now. We will continue later,' the Pakistani major remarked as he abruptly exited Hamir's room.

Hamir smiled to himself. He was not tired at all. The major just needed an excuse to leave. He had probably seen what he had come to see.

But what the Pakistani major said caught Hamir's attention. He finally understood why the Pakistanis believed he was a commando.

He had joined his battalion just before the war. The only personal information the men had about their company commander was that he had returned from abroad just a few days prior to the war. The fact that he had been an instructor at the Nigerian Defence Academy at Kaduna was known to only a select few.

During their interrogation his men had possibly revealed

that their company commander had been abroad; for some reason the Pakistanis automatically assumed that he had joined his battalion after having attended the Rangers Course in the US, which was a renowned course subscribed by Indian infantry officers of that era.

The nature of Hamir's task at Daruchhian, the tough fight he had given before being captured and his physical appearance had all added up to give the impression to the Pakistanis that he was a commando.

While this was good for his ego the downside was the added attention he was subjected to as a prisoner. The overcautiousness with which they handled him left him with little privacy and was often extremely suffocating.

It was almost the end of February when one day the nurse on duty barged into his room. She was smiling.

'Sir, we have received orders to shift you today. You will be joining the other officers. No more isolation for you!'

'Really?' Hamir couldn't believe it. If what she said was true it was indeed good news. It would be wonderful to join his Indian colleagues.

'Yes, sir, it's true!' she insisted, and she was right.

Hamir had missed out on the first repatriation carried out on 25 February. Now that he was an officially acknowledged POW the hospital authorities had apparently taken a decision to put him up with the other Indian officers at CMH, Rawalpindi.

After breakfast he was formally informed about the decision to move him to the officers' ward. The room attendant helped him pack his meagre belongings and then escorted him to it. He had been allotted a room which could accommodate up to four officers. When he entered the room he found two Indian officers awaiting him.

The first, a tall, well-built officer stood at the door. He wore an eyepatch over his left eye. They shook hands. 'Welcome, Hamir, I am Major S.S. Choudhury, 4 Grenadiers.'

'Thank you, have we met before?' Hamir said.

'No, I don't think so. And this is Major Surve,' he remarked gesturing towards the other officer. Major Surve seemed wounded too. His right elbow was bandaged.

'Hello, I am A.D. Surve, Third Nine.'[24]

'Appa Saheb Dada Saheb Surve,' Choudhury added, smiling.

Hamir nodded. 'What a coincidence! I met Second Lieutenant Ganga Ram Chaudhary of your unit too here in the hospital,' he remarked.

Of the four beds in the room two were vacant. Hamir placed his belongings on the unoccupied bed next to Surve. He spent a few minutes setting his things while the other too watched silently.

By the time the mid-morning tea was served the three Indians were conversing like old friends. One of the first things they realized was that they had passed out from the Indian Military Academy, Dehradun in the same year. During their training at IMA they had belonged to different battalions, hence they hadn't gotten to know each other too well. While Hamir and Choudhury were married, Surve was single.

Major Choudhury was a simple officer and a little reserved. His behaviour and demeanour were very much like that of Hamir. Surve on the other hand was an extrovert who would lighten up the atmosphere with his antics and light-hearted banter. He was quite popular with the nurses with whom he would joke around, indulging in a fair bit of mutual leg-pulling. The three of them together proved to be excellent company to each other.

Meanwhile a new surgical specialist, Colonel Mehmood Hassan, had joined CMH, Rawalpindi on posting a few days back. Colonel Hassan had an excellent professional reputation. Immediately on his arrival the commandant requested him, as well as the eye specialist, to take a look at the Indian officers who were due for a medical review. Hamir, Choudhury and Surve were subjected to a detailed examination after which the doctors submitted their reports to the commandant. In the surgical specialist's opinion Hamir and Surve would require additional surgeries. The eye specialist concluded that there was nothing more that could be done for Choudhury. There was no requirement to retain him at the hospital and accordingly he was recommended for immediate discharge. The commandant agreed with him. Choudhury was discharged and transferred to a POW camp a few days later.

Since both Hamir and Surve were not confined to their beds they were allowed to walk outside in the corridor adjacent to their room. While they walked they were closely supervised by two sentries, located at either end of the corridor.

It felt wonderful to be outdoors. Observing life on the outside provided them a sense of normalcy. They enjoyed observing the normal hustle and bustle of the military camps. An occasional working party toiling away repairing a road or a broken wall. A small garden located about 700 yards away where every evening one would find happy children playing under their mothers' watchful eyes, as they would in any town in India. Seeing the happy families Hamir would often grow nostalgic thinking about home and the happy days he had spent in Nigeria with his small family.

One Sunday evening Hamir and Surve were surprised to see Colonel Hassan in their room. Apparently, since their surgeries were scheduled the next day, he had come over to explain what the procedures would involve.

Surve had lost a large amount of flesh near his elbow. His hand would be surgically attached to the skin of his stomach. This arrangement was to remain in place for three to four weeks until the skin regenerated and covered the wounds near his elbow.

As for Hamir the surgical specialist would address the damage to his radial nerve, due to which he had developed a medical condition known as wrist drop. He had lost the ability to clench his fist or to grip objects firmly. Tendons and part of a nerve would be grafted from other parts of his body and skilfully re-attached to his arm.

The operations were carried out the very next day and both of them were successful. They would now have to wait patiently for their wounds to heal.

A few days later an ICRC representative paid Hamir a visit as he was walking outdoors. He seemed concerned seeing

Hamir's heavily bandaged hand. However, after he explained that he had undergone surgery to improve the mobility of his hand the man was satisfied. He was also happy to learn that the authorities had provided him newspapers and a transistor after the last ICRC visit. He left wishing Hamir all the best for a speedy and complete recovery.

An ICRC delegate visiting Hamir at CMH, Rawalpindi. Source: International Review of the Red Cross, no. 134 (May 1972), p. 290.

Hamir and Surve were like two peas in a pod, having undergone similar operations and sharing the same room. Hamir's bandaged hand was supported by a simple sling, therefore he was free to move about. Surve though wasn't as lucky. His bandages restricted his mobility and he remained confined to his bed making him the butt of jokes of the giggly nurses. One day he was in a particularly dour mood. The moment he saw the nurse he complained.

'Arre, sister! Mujhe yeh punishment kyun di ja rahi hai. Tang ho gaya hoon lete lete!' he said, frustrated. *Oh sister! Why am I being punished? I am tired of lying in bed!*

'Kyunki aap har waqt badmashi karte rehte ho! Operation karna hi aapko control karne ka tarika tha. Aapke kaan toh nahin khench sakte the na?' she replied, amused. *Because you are always up to mischief. The operation was the only way to put a leash on you. We couldn't pull your ears, could we?*

Hamir joined the fun. 'Haan, aur mere kaan to pehle hi ek mohtarma ne khench rakhe hain!' he remarked. *Yes and my ears have already been pulled by a woman.*

'What?' the nurse exclaimed. 'Ye kab hua?' *When did this happen?*

Surve seemed confused too. He looked towards Hamir waiting for an explanation.

'It happened a long time back in Ladakh,' Hamir replied, and he was transported back to the year 1963 when he was stationed at Karu in Ladakh.

February 1963. Karu, Ladakh

Major S.R. Das, Hamir's company commander was beaming when Hamir met him in his tent that served as the ad hoc office of Delta Company 2 Grenadiers.

'Hello, tiger. I have got some good news! There's an assignment for you which I know you will enjoy,' he remarked.

'That's wonderful, sir,' Hamir replied. 'And what am I to do?'

'You are going on a two-week reconnaissance patrol to the Tanglang La—the Tanglang mountain pass.'

'Really?' Hamir was excited.

'Yes. Please speak to the adjutant immediately. He will brief you. Thereafter you are to meet the CO tomorrow,' Major Das replied.

The purpose of the patrol became clear once Hamir spoke to the adjutant. A road was proposed to be constructed between Leh and Manali.[25] Hamir would carry out the very first reconnaissance for the road from Karu to the Tanglang La located at a height of 5,328 metres (17,480 feet). The two-week patrol required Hamir to select his team and work out the administrative details.

He immediately got to work. It was February and reasonably cold. He selected the most physically fit personnel from the battalion and together they planned every aspect in minute detail.

They would look for shelter in the villages enroute but would cater for tentage in case of an emergency. The need for rations had to be balanced against their load carrying capacity, given the high altitude that they would be traversing through. They had been allotted a few ponies and mules to help them carry their supplies. A couple of interpreters were hired to accompany them and obviously Norbu the interpreter had to be an integral member of the patrol.

The commanding officer Lt Col J. Nazareth briefed the patrol about what was expected of the patrol. They were required to gather information about the terrain and villages enroute. Although the main purpose of the patrol was to help plan the future road any other information would be welcome. He wished them well and they were soon on their way.

The route followed the River Indus until a village called Upshi, where they would spend their first night and marry up with Norbu and his team of labourers and horses for the trek ahead.

The next day the patrol trekked to village Miru along a deep gorge with a precipitous, sharp mountainside along the route. As there were no suitable camping sites enroute, camp was planned at Miru itself. It was a physically demanding trek and by evening they had reached the outskirts of Miru. When the villagers observed the approaching party they fled in fright. They had rarely seen human beings come that way. Hamir ordered Norbu to proceed ahead and announce the purpose of their visit.

Norbu was able to reassure the villagers and when the main party arrived at the village the Gaon Burha received them at the entrance of the village. An impressive old man, he was extremely tall and sported a long, grey beard. He spoke in a measured tone and appeared to be a particularly wise man. Norbu did the talking and Hamir and his party were allowed to camp in a part of the village where a couple of unutilized hut-like structures were available.

After they had settled in for the night the village headman approached the interpreter with an unusual request. One of the village ponies had contracted rabies and was in immense agony. It was impossible for anyone to even attempt approaching it let alone touch it. With no treatment available the headman requested Hamir's party put it out of its misery.

It was an unusual task but when Hamir saw the condition of the pony he realized that it was the best course of action for the poor animal. He gave the task to one of his men who used his .303 rifle to put the pony to rest.

The relieved headman thanked them profusely and thereafter Hamir's party was accepted by the villagers as friends.

Hamir spent the next few days moving around the area diligently completing their assigned tasks. They trekked right up to village Artse, obtaining a very good idea of the Artse Valley from where the Tanglang La was visible at a distance. However, at Artse the villagers wouldn't allow them beyond the village. February was a treacherous month to climb up the snowclad Tanglang La and the villagers' advice was absolutely appropriate. Hamir decided to follow their advice. He returned to Karu and submitted a detailed report to the Brigade HQ.

The report was well received. It was the first time that such a detailed report had been made available. Based on the report a team of veterinarians was dispatched to Miru and Artse in a gesture of friendship whereby they would treat the animals affected by rabies.

After a month or so Hamir's CO, Lt Col Nazareth expressed the desire to visit Miru. Nazareth had received his posting and was to leave the sector shortly. Before he left he was keen to experience the local way of life which Hamir had written about while filing his report.

Hamir was tasked to accompany him and together they left for Miru with a party of about thirty men. On their way they came across a group of mountain goats which they promptly hunted down. The efforts yielded an addition of two goats to their kitty as they approached the village.

This time when they approached the village they received a warm welcome by the villagers chanting 'Juley, juley, juley'. The tall village headman approached Hamir and welcomed him like a long-lost friend, while Nazareth looked amused. The headman conveyed his gratitude to Hamir for sending the veterinarians who had miraculously saved their animals. Hamir was now a local hero and considered as a person who could make anything possible. Nazareth gifted the mountain goats that Hamir had shot to the village headman as a gesture of friendship, which he graciously accepted.

A celebratory feast was organized and Nazareth and Hamir were to be hosted as the village headman's honoured guests. In the evening both of them were welcomed into the headman's modest hut in the traditional manner. They were ushered into the dining area and offered seats on the woollen rugs placed on the wooden floor. They sat together in a small circle.

After a few minutes of polite conversation two young women, elaborately dressed in traditional wear, apparently the hostesses, arrived with a jug of chhang, the local beer-like brew, which they dexterously poured into small mugs placed besides the guests. Once they were done the beautiful women withdrew to the background and stood behind the guests. There was a pregnant pause as the hostesses waited expectantly. All eyes were now on the CO who blushed self-consciously as he glanced towards Hamir, looking for a cue. Hamir nonchalantly picked up the small cup. 'Juley!' he said as he gulped down the drink; it was the only word he knew in the local language. Nazareth followed tentatively. 'Juley!' he went, and the hosts joined him. He could only manage a small sip, barely disguising his involuntary gagging. It tasted sour, like nothing he had drunk before.

The hostesses noticed with appreciation that Hamir had emptied his cup. They returned a second time and refilled his cup. Now Hamir was a bit hesitant, he needed to go slow. He didn't want to lose control of himself in the presence of his CO. The ladies returned and stood beside them inconspicuously. Before Hamir and Nazareth could realize what they were doing, the ladies bent down, caught hold of their guests' ears and gently tugged at them. Hamir and Nazareth were taken aback and didn't know how to react. Only much later, when Norbu explained that it was a local custom, did they enjoy a hearty laugh.

~

'So that's when my ear was pulled by a beautiful lady,' Hamir said, smiling. 'And you should have seen my CO Lt Col Nazareth's face when his ear was pulled. He just didn't know what hit him.'

'That type of pulling I wouldn't mind, sister,' Surve remarked. 'Yahan toh meri leg-pulling hi chalti hai!' he added. *Out here it's just my leg that's being pulled all the time!* The three of them burst out laughing.

After a few weeks when their bandages were removed both Surve and Hamir found out that they were much better. Colonel Hassan had done a truly professional job.

April 1972

Surve and Hamir were excellent company to each other. While Hamir was reserved and reticent, Surve was funny and gregarious. If one felt low the other would pull him out of his dour mood by narrating a funny anecdote, singing a song or playing a mischievous prank.

To add to their company was a generator operator who was always on duty during the daylight hours. A large generator shed was positioned just across their room and its inquisitive operator would spend more time sitting on the wall separating the generator shed and the ward than the generator shed itself. Whenever there was a power outage the short distance between their wall and the generator shed allowed the operator to run across and switch on the generator double-quick. The arrangement was most convenient.

Forever inquisitive, he would innocently engage them in conversation, unrestrained by protocol, being a civilian employee of the Military Engineering Service. His chats would range from local politics to interesting stories or anecdotes from the newspaper. He added spice to their conversations which made them outrageous and funny.

Life was definitely much better ever since Hamir had shifted into the officers' ward. Besides the company of Surve and others they were provided newspapers and were given a transistor. The icing on the cake were the numerous packages they received from India. Now that there were just the two of them left at Rawalpindi the packages were all theirs for the keeping.

Each package would be opened with as much enthusiasm as a child would exhibit on his birthday. The contents were always a mystery and guessing what goodies the packages contained became a game and bets would be wagered.

They contained an assortment of things ranging from shaving accessories to toiletries, biscuits and other eats. Often religious books were received, which were considered essential for their spiritual and mental well-being. Even for someone not too spiritually inclined as Hamir the books provided something to read.

Thankfully by now most of the staff and administration at the hospital had realized that Hamir was a Rajput and not a Sikh. There were now a fair number of Hindu religious books in his bedside locker while a couple of religious photographs of Hindu gods and goddesses adorned his windowsill. These pictures would invariably be the topic of conversation with visitors, who wished to know who they were and what they represented.

Partition was still a relatively recent event and the older among the staff had a fair idea of Hindu traditions and festivals. They would recall the happy times spent celebrating Hindu and Muslim festivals with their neighbours and friends. There was mutual respect for all religions and every festive occasion was a celebration of life.

Late in the evening one day the subedar major paid them a visit.

'Sahab, this is my last visit,' he remarked.

'Why, sahab?' Hamir asked. 'Are you being posted out?'

'No, no, sahab. I am being posted out for good. I superannuate at the end of this month. I am leaving CMH tomorrow for the retirement formalities and paperwork,' the SM informed him.

'Oh! Is that so? I wish you had told us earlier. We could have organized a tea party for you at least.'

Hamir meant what he said. The man had always been nice. The least they could do was offer him a cup of tea.

The subedar major smiled. 'No way, sir. You are our guests. How can I let my guests throw *me* a party? I am supposed to be your host.'

Hamir could sense a hint of emotion in his voice.

'Sahab, if I, or any of the staff have not treated you well—I apologize. Please forgive us,' he said in all sincerity.

'Don't say that, sahab, on the contrary you have been very nice. You were key to making our life bearable here in Pakistan. Our morale has remained high because of your efforts. Thank you very much for everything,' Hamir told him.

He walked up to the subedar major and shook his hands. Surve, who was listening to their conversation, totally agreed. The subedar major was a fine man. A wonderful example of the institution of subedar majors in the army.

'Sahab, I have a request,' the SM said.

'Sure, sahab. What can I do for you?' Hamir asked.

'Do you have a copy of the Gita in English?' The subedar major was referring to the Hindu religious book which Hamir had in his possession, thanks to the ICRC parcels.

'Sorry, sahab, the only copy I have is in Hindi. But I promise you if I ever get a copy in English I shall send it to you.' Hamir was intrigued by the SM's unusual request. 'But tell me SM sahab, what will you do with it?'

'Sahab, many generations ago, we were Hindus too. I want my children to know what our scriptures looked like. Inshallah, there's something in it for my children to learn.'

His words took them by surprise. They were humbled by the wisdom of the man. *The world would definitely be a better place if the youth of both countries shared the wisdom of this man*, Hamir thought as they bid him farewell.

June 1972

It was a blazing hot afternoon and with nothing better to do Surve and Hamir had tuned in to the BBC's running commentary of the Ashes Trophy match between England and Australia. It was the fifth and final day at Manchester. Australia were struggling to chase 342 runs required to win the first test match. In both the innings Tony Greig had been England's hero while batting as well as bowling.

Greig was bowling to John Gleeson, the last Australian batsman. He bowled a gem of a ball and John Gleeson was bowled out. England had won the first test match by eighty-nine runs.

Surve and Hamir who had been siding with England for no particular reason, cheered loudly, especially since their sentry was rooting for Australia. The sentry, crestfallen, commented—'Koi baat nahin. December mein dekhenge India inka samna kaise karte hain!' *Don't worry, let's see how India handles England in December!*

He was referring to the India–England series scheduled to be held in December 1972 in India.

'Arre, kya tumne hamare Gavaskar aur Vishwanath ka nahin suna? England ki baja denge hamare batsmen!' Surve replied. *Haven't you heard of Gavaskar and Vishwanath? They will sort England out!*

The banter between Surve and the sentry continued till late in the evening. Each Indian and English player was discussed threadbare. What would actually happen in India only time would tell.

Amidst all the discussion Hamir remained quiet. The talk of cricket and sports always reminded him of his father. A sports enthusiast, Kalyan Singh would often be glued to his radio early in the morning or late at night. He could visualize his father walking in the fields with his pocket radio following the Ashes match as they had been doing that afternoon.

That night as he lay down he missed his parents dearly. He wondered what they would be doing. He imagined his father sitting on his favourite chair in the open courtyard of his haveli waiting for his dinner, while his mother would be hunched over the fireplace cooking his favourite dish, a delicious aroma filling the entire courtyard. Hamir missed his parents and their memories pained his heart.

He realized he hadn't even said a proper goodbye to them. *I wish I had spent some more time with them before leaving for the war*, he thought. He wondered whether he would ever get a chance to meet them again.

Bhagwanpura, Rajasthan

It had been over three years since his retirement and Maj Gen Kalyan Singh was living the kind of life he desired, post retirement. It was precisely for this reason that despite the many offers for work he had received in Delhi and Jaipur he had chosen a peaceful retired life in his paternal village, Bhagwanpura.

His decision to stay away from the limelight was not hard to understand given the remarkable and eventful life he had spent in the Indian Army.

An impressive six-foot-two in stature, Kalyan Singh joined 16 Cavalry as a Sowar. Soon thereafter he was selected as an officer cadet and underwent training at Kitchener College, Nowgong[26] before being commissioned in 2 Indian Field Regiment in 1940.

During the Second World War he was captured by the Germans in North Africa while fighting the forces of Erwin Rommel as part of the 3rd Indian Motor Brigade. Among his fellow prisoners were Major P.P. Kumaramangalam (later Chief of Army Staff of the Indian Army) and Major Tikka Khan (later Chief of Staff of the Pakistan Army).

They escaped together from the Italian POW Camp Number 63 located at Aversa, Italy only to be recaptured later and sent to Germany, where they remained till the end of the war. Tikka Khan and Kalyan Singh spent a year together attending the Long Gunnery Staff Course (LGSC) at The Royal School of Artillery, Larkhill, England.

Major General Kalyan Singh (right), then GOC 8 Mountain Division.

During the 1962 Sino-Indian war 'the steady and great Rajput warrior Brigadier Kalyan Singh'[27] commanded 4 Artillery Brigade in an infantry role. He was awarded a VSM Class 1 (renamed Param Vishisht Seva Medal, PVSM, in 1967) for bravery.[28] He went on to command 8 Mountain Division, and when General Kumaramangalam became the Chief of Army Staff, he appointed Kalyan Singh as the Military Secretary. Though approved for his next rank Kalyan Singh retired in March 1969 for want of a vacancy for promotion.

In the years prior to his retirement he had spent every annual leave in the village to oversee construction of a modern

Major General Kalyan Singh in NEFA.

annexe to his haveli. This was to be his personal living quarters cum office where he would keep his collection of books, magazines and files. Along with its construction he had also carried out repair and maintenance of the remaining part of the haveli. Its magnificent hall, full of interesting artefacts and photos from his travels became a talking point. Villagers would seek opportunities to catch a glimpse of the Naga spears, shields and other such exotic artefacts.

Kalyan Singh himself was a much sought-after person. His magnificent white haveli, conveniently located on the main highway, became a favourite pit stop for politicians and other notable individuals keen to spread their influence in the area. He took advantage of such visits as he would extract promises from the VIPs for the improvement of infrastructure in the village.

As a result of his efforts a number of essential services came up at Bhagwanpura. It was among the first of the villages in the region to have its own hospital, dispensary, primary school, water works and community TV. His settling down at

Bhagwanpura had turned out to be a boon for the inhabitants of the village and it prospered.

The haveli had turned into a durbar with locals seeking his counsel and advice. To them he was a problem solver who could get things moving. His word was authority and a mere mention that 'General sahab' had so desired would elicit an immediate response. He walked the streets of the village like a king with well-wishers in tow. He was no less a general to the locals who were to him no less than his soldiers. In that sense he didn't really feel he had retired from the army.

It was a warm May evening and a large crowd had gathered at the haveli to have a look at his crop of freshly harvested onions. For the first time in the village, Kalyan Singh had grown onions. It had turned out to be a bumper crop and promised good returns. The local farmers looked at the large pile of onions in wonder.

The onions had completely occupied the wire-mesh enclosed verandah located in the anterior portion of the house. A group of women were at work packing the onions into the gunny sacks while labourers stowed the gunny sacks in neat rows, one over the other. The pungent smell of the onions was overpowering but no one seemed to mind.

Kalyan Singh sat on his muddha under the neem tree, next to his outhouse, proudly watching the proceedings and accepting the many compliments.

Among his visitors was a retired soldier who stayed on to chat with General sahab. They conversed for some time over a cup of tea and the topic turned to Hamir. Everyone in the village knew that Hamir was a POW in the war and the retired soldier politely inquired about Hamir's well-being.

'General sahab, kya Hamir banna wapas aa jayenge?' he asked. *General sahab, will Hamir come back?*

'Kyun nahin, jaroor!' Kalyan Singh replied. *Why not, definitely!*

'I believe many POWs of the previous wars have never returned. Besides, if they come back they are often harassed for allowing themselves to be captured.'

'I am sure they will all come back. After all, we hold many more Pakistani POWs than they do! Besides, no soldier voluntarily surrenders. They become POWs because of the peculiar circumstances, which you and I sitting in the comforts of our houses have no idea about. I was a POW during the World War, don't you know?' Kalyan Singh replied, slightly annoyed.

'Yes, sir, I know. But you know how people talk. All of us are hoping to welcome Hamir sahab back as a hero,' he added.

After the soldier left Kalyan Singh remained distracted for the rest of the day. He had his dinner quietly and retired to his annexe. What the soldier had inadvertently mentioned had got him thinking.

What if Hamir doesn't come back? How will Laxmi and the kids manage? Kalyan's aunt was a child widow and she lived a lonely life with them in Kalyan's haveli. *Is Laxmi destined to a similar future?*

Sleepless, he walked out towards the haud—water reservoir—located in the adjoining field. *What if he returns and the authorities find that he had given up without a fight? That would bring terrible shame to the family.*

He was really disturbed now and he walked aimlessly amidst his fields, trying to tire himself out. *If only I had spent more time with him before he left for battle*, he thought.

He did care for Hamir, as any father would. However, overt expression of love wasn't a done thing in traditional Rajput families. In that regard Kalyan had been old-fashioned.

Will I ever get a chance to meet Hamir again? he wondered. *Will I be able to show him that I really care for him?*

He felt helpless and alone that night. A veteran of many wars Kalyan was plagued with worry about his son and what the future would hold for his illustrious family.

By the time Kalyan returned to his bedroom it was way past midnight. A hypertension patient, he would sometimes take sleeping pills to sleep away high blood pressure. For the first time in his life he needed sleeping pills for reasons other than hypertension.

The Road to Recovery

Command Military Hospital, Rawalpindi

There were whispers in early June at the CMH, Rawalpindi of an imminent exchange of prisoners. This time two wounded Indian POWs would be repatriated. This was welcome news as only Hamir and Surve remained.

Hamir though was not so sure. The last time prisoners had been repatriated he had been disappointed. He didn't want to think too much about it and remained somewhat circumspect. Surve on the other hand was optimistic and certain that both of them would finally be home. Curiously, an extra bed had also been placed in their room suggesting the arrival of another Indian POW.

Around midday the next day a tall, well-built officer, clad in salwar kameez, donning a smart pair of dark glasses entered their room.

'Good morning, gentlemen, how are you?' he said. The voice seemed familiar.

'Oho! It's you, Chou. Welcome back!' Hamir said. There was no fooling him.

'Arre! You guys have recognized me!' Major S.S. Choudhury seemed surprised.

'Absolutely. What did you think, we wouldn't recognize you just because you've filled out?' Hamir commented. 'Looks like the prison food has suited you.'

'Haan yaar, mota ho gaya hoon!' Choudhury replied. *Yes, I have become fat.* The three of them had a hearty laugh. Choudhury had put on weight and it actually suited him. He looked healthy and fit.

Now that there were three wounded POWs, it was obvious that one of them was not destined to return to India, if only two were to be repatriated.

'See, I told you, Surve, I would be left behind. Choudhury and you are headed home, you just wait and see.'

'Why do you say that, brother? Since they have brought Chou here, he will definitely be going. But as for the second POW it could be either of us,' Surve countered.

'Let's see what tomorrow brings for us. I guess our destiny will decide,' Hamir replied.

Shortly thereafter an officer arrived to complete their documentation. He didn't indicate who was to be repatriated. All three were told to be packed and ready to proceed the next day.

'Hamir, I will write a letter to my parents and give it to you. You do the same and hand it over to me. Whoever goes home will deliver it to the family of the one left behind,' Surve suggested.

'Forget it, yaar, you are going. Just tell my parents and wife that I am well, OK?' Hamir insisted.

'Theek hai, bhai. If you say so,' Surve replied.

At eleven the next morning the names of the POWs to be repatriated were announced. Major S.S. Choudhury and Major A.D. Surve were chosen to return to India.

On hearing the announcement Surve became emotional. He pleaded with the commandant that he be allowed to stay and that Hamir should be repatriated. After all he was a bachelor while Hamir was married and had a family to return to. His requests fell on deaf ears as the commandant expressed his helplessness. The orders were from the higher authorities and there was no scope for any change.

When it was time to leave Surve and Hamir shook hands. Surve hugged Hamir with tears in his eyes.

'I will miss you, my friend. I wish they had let you go instead,' he lamented.

'Don't worry, brother. I am sure my time will come too. Do remember to convey my well-being home.'

'Yes, I will,' said Surve solemnly.

Surve and Choudhury were escorted out, leaving Hamir behind. As Hamir returned to his now vacant room the sound of his footsteps seemed to echo much louder than before. He was now the sole Indian soldier in Command Military Hospital, Rawalpindi.

~

The Road to Recovery

Now that he was alone the other patients in the hospital and the staff indulged him. The staff would hover around him longer than required. There was no end to visitors as patients from the neighbouring wards wouldn't leave him alone for too long. Besides, the second POW exchange had ensured a fresh lot of inquisitive officers who would interact with him from time to time.

Ever since he had been admitted at Rawalpindi, Hamir had been attended to by two nurses. The senior of the two nurses belonged to Rawalpindi. She was middle-aged and had a motherly attitude. The other, Bilkish Rana, was a young, strikingly pretty Rajput Muslim woman who belonged to Lyallpur. Both nurses were professional and caring.

Soon after Hamir became the lone occupant of the officers' ward the senior nurse was posted out. As a result the responsibility of Hamir's care was left to Bilkish Rana, who would fuss over him like a younger sister. Being Rajputs—albeit born into different faiths—they shared a common ancestry and that resulted in a special bond between the two of them.

Hamir now found himself meeting a large number of Rajput Muslims, almost as if they had taken it upon themselves to ensure that he never felt alone. Among his visitors were the eye specialist, Major Rathore, some other doctors and fellow patients. They would talk about their lives in Pakistan, the similarity of their customs and marriages. They would often bring him fruits and other eatables. Hamir was indebted to them as they made life bearable when it could have become a particularly lonely time for him in Pakistan.

One evening Hamir found Bilkish in her civvies. He was surprised.

'What happened, sister? Why are you in this dress?' he asked.

'Sir, I am posted out. I am leaving for Lahore,' Bilkish told him.

'Achha...' Hamir couldn't hide his disappointment. He would definitely miss her.

'It was nice knowing you, sir. I hope you return to your family soon, inshallah,' she continued.

'I will miss you, sister. You looked after me with care. May God be with you!' Hamir replied.

'Sir, I have a request.'

'Sure, sister, please tell me.'

'When you return to India, please look after my fiance.'

'Fiance?' Hamir replied, surprised.

'Yes, sir. My fiance is an army doctor, Captain Shaukat Rana.[29] He was serving in East Pakistan when the war commenced. All I know is that he is now a POW. As to where he is, I have no idea.'

Hamir was surprised, Bilkish had never shared this information with him. She had always been calm and good-natured. If she ever had any anxiety due to her fiance's captivity, she never showed it.

'Oh, sister, why didn't you tell me earlier? I would have told Surve or Choudhury to locate him. You would have all the details by now,' Hamir said.

'Sir, I informed Major Surve before he left. Though all our soldiers who have returned from India mentioned that they were well looked after, I still worry about him.'

'You needn't worry, sister. I am certain he is fine. Doctors are normally asked to work in the hospital to treat their own soldiers. He would be treating Pakistanis. I promise you sister that if I am fortunate enough to be repatriated I shall find Captain Shaukat Rana. He will be well looked after, we owe it to you.' He meant every word he said.

'Thank you. I feel much better hearing that, bhaijaan.' There were tears in her eyes. It was the first time that she had referred to Hamir as her brother. It was the last he saw of Bilkish Rana. She would be missed.

~

Hamir was resting on his bed one day when Major Hameed walked into his room. He had been a regular visitor ever since he was repatriated. However, he hadn't visited for quite a while.

'It's been a while, Hameed.'

'Yes, sir, long time indeed. How are you?'

'I am fine, thank you. What brings you here today?'

'Sir, when we met last time you had mentioned that you had fought in the Poonch Sector, am I right?' Hameed inquired.

'Yes, that's correct.'

'I have a favour to ask you!'

'Go ahead, Hameed.'

'Sir, there is a lady who has come to meet you. Can I let her in?'

Hamir thought for a while. It must be one of the two ladies he had met in hospital immediately after his capture. The ones who had fed him 'keenu'. They had been nice to him and meeting them again would be fun. 'Sure, I have no problem as long as your guys give permission,' he replied.

'That's wonderful, sir. I have taken permission; I will just get her over.'

Hameed exited the room. A short while later a young girl entered the room. She couldn't have been more than four to five years old and her face was lit with excitement. The moment she entered the room she turned back towards the door.

'No, mama, not here, we have entered the wrong room. This is uncle's room!' the girl seemed disappointed.

'No, baby. This is the right room, *this is* the Hindu uncle,' Major Hameed remarked. The girl's mother had also entered the room and now stood beside Hameed.

'But he is not a Hindu, mama, yeh toh hamare jaise uncle hain!' she insisted. *He is like our uncles.* Apparently she had been brought up with a caricature of what a Hindu looked like and Hamir didn't fit that image.

'Sabeena! Shh. Please ab tum chup bhi raho.' *Keep quiet now!* The mother then looked towards Hamir and nodded politely.

'Salaam alaikum, janab,' she said softly, almost inaudible.

'Alaikum salaam,' Hamir replied.

'Sir, let me introduce you, she is my cousin sister,' Hameed interjected.

'Oh, I see!'

'Her husband has been missing in action since the commencement of the war. He had participated in an attack near Poonch on 4–5 December.'

'Sorry to hear that,' Hamir remarked.

'She was wondering if you know anything about him, since you were at Poonch.'

'He was CO of an Azad Kashmir Battalion,' the lady added. 'Did you ever hear of him, sir? Could you tell me anything?'

'Let me think… Just give me a moment.' Hamir remained silent for a little while as he gathered his thoughts, recollecting the events of early December 1971 when he had spent some time in Poonch.

3 December 1971. Poonch Sector

The war had commenced. 14 Grenadiers, who were at Sarol, were given orders to move towards Poonch and occupy a defensive position ahead of Bhimber Gali, near Poonch. It was believed that the Pakistanis were planning an attack there. One company worth of men was left behind at Sarol while the remaining battalion prepared for the move.

The move began at 19:30 hours and by the time the battalion arrived at their new location it was midnight. They had no time to rest and remained busy throughout the night preparing their defences. By first light they were well prepared, confident that they would be able to take on the enemy.

4 December

Poonch town had always been an important target for the enemy but its well-prepared defences made its capture extremely challenging. On the other hand, Thanpir, a mountain feature just behind Poonch was sparsely occupied and provided an easier option. But to capture Thanpir the enemy would need to infiltrate through Indian territory.

Thanpir overlooked Kalai Bridge, a strategically important bridge on the road to Poonch town. Its capture would interfere in the movement of reinforcements and supplies to Poonch.

On the morning of the fourth of December reports were received that Kalai Bridge had been captured by Pakistani commandos who had infiltrated into Indian territory. Thanpir was also reported to have been captured by a POK Battalion.

33 Mountain Brigade, which had been moved into the area the previous night, was ordered to recapture Kalai Bridge and Thanpir as soon as possible.

13 Mahar, an infantry battalion of the 33 Mountain Brigade, was tasked to capture Thanpir and 9 Para Commando was allotted to them for this task.

As far as 14 Grenadiers was concerned Hamir's company was to prevent reinforcements or supplies from reaching the Pakistani troops on Thanpir. To carry out this task they selected a position at Gutrian from where the Pakistanis had infiltrated. From this position they would be able to cut off reinforcements and even the route of escape, should the Pakistanis be forced back.

Hamir was to follow 13 Mahar along the road until the Kalai Bridge. A gurdwara close to the Kalai Bridge was the designated point from where Hamir's company would move to its own location.

Accordingly they followed 13 Mahar amid sounds of heavy shelling along the entire front. Exchange of fire could be heard from the upper reaches of Thanpir as well. Hamir's company reached the gurdwara without incident. They now switched to their own route along the nala and arrived at their chosen position at 21:00 hours. A short while later they were ready and waiting for the enemy.

While Hamir's company waited 13 Mahar and 9 Para Commando were fighting the battle to recapture Thanpir. At about 01:00 hours Hamir received orders to return to the gurdwara. Apparently the operations on Thanpir had gone off well and it was felt that Hamir's company was no longer required. They moved immediately and were able to reach the gurdwara just as dawn was breaking.

5 December

It had been a physically demanding twenty-four hours for Hamir and his company. Now that they had arrived at the gurdwara Hamir decided to allow the men to rest for a while. But before that they would need to clean their weapons and take stock of their stores so that they were prepared for the next operation. By the time they finished it was time for lunch. After lunch Hamir allowed the company to rest until 18:00 hours, when they would be passed fresh orders. Hamir used the time to freshen up, and after lunch, settled in for a nap.

He had slept for some time when in the evening he was woken up by the sound of the war cries of the Para Commandos. They had returned to the gurdwara which was their base. Morale was understandably high as together with 13 Mahar they had recaptured Thanpir.

Hamir decided to meet the Commandos. He was keen to know what had transpired atop Thanpir. By the time he reached their location the Commandos had dispersed. However, he found a young captain sitting on a camp stool, enjoying his refreshments. Hamir introduced himself and requested the captain to narrate what had happened at Thanpir. The captain obliged and Hamir listened in rapt attention for almost twenty minutes until he came to the end of his narrative—'...and sir, we got the Commanding Officer[30] as well. Very tall, maybe six-foot-two or so.'

'Where's he now?' Hamir interjected.

'He is with his maker, sir, where he deserves to be! He was a huge guy, sir. Couldn't manage to get him down on our own, used our porters.' The captain then opened his backpack and pulled out a black leather wallet and a plastic bag.

'These are my trophies, sir, I found them in the dead man's pocket.' The captain flipped the wallet open showing Hamir the Pakistani currency notes and the few photographs it contained.

Meanwhile the captain drew out a taweez from the plastic bag and wrenched the small metallic cylinder open and a piece of paper fell out. He unfolded the paper and showed Hamir the mystic characters inscribed on it.

'See, sir, this was what he was wearing around his arm. Even this could not save the poor guy's life.' He was not done yet. He put his hand into the plastic bag and this time took out a chequebook.

'Here, sir, take a look,' he said, handing over the chequebook to Hamir. 'If you look carefully at the blank cheques below you will be able to see the imprint of the last cheque he signed. It reads Rs 2,000/- and is signed on 2 December.'

What he said was true, the imprint was easily visible. Intrigued, Hamir examined the chequebook. The address of the account holder was written on the inside of the cover page. It read: 17,[31] The Mall, Lahore Cantonment.

'I wonder why he was required to carry his chequebook to battle. Must be clearing his dues before the battle. Real gentleman, don't you think, sir?' the captain commented sarcastically.

Hamir didn't like the idea of the young captain mocking a dead soldier. The Commandos had no doubt done a good job and their bravado was understandable. But the young officer needed to be reined in.

'Captain, well done. You and your men have done well indeed. But I have a suggestion as an elder brother?' Hamir said.

'Thank you, sir, and what's the suggestion, sir?'

'Captain, always respect a dead soldier, even if he is an enemy.'

'Absolutely, sir, I totally agree. I didn't mean to disrespect the man. My apologies if I gave you that impression. He gave his life for his country. My men all felt for him and that's why we got him down and gave him the last rites he deserves,' the captain replied, embarrassed.

Hamir was relieved. For a moment he had thought that the young officer had got carried away by his success.

'Well done, Captain, that's what I expected from any professional soldier,' Hamir remarked.

'Thank you, sir. We buried him here, near the gurdwara. We felt it was an appropriate resting place.'

The commanding officer of the POK Battalion (or Azad Kashmir Battalion as the lady had referred to it) had been laid to rest behind the Dera Nangali Gurdwara, Poonch at the banks of Drungali Nallah.

Command Military Hospital, Rawalpindi

'Do you know anything about my husband, sir?'

Hamir was still engrossed in his memories of Poonch. The lady's voice brought him back to the present.

'Yes, I think so,' Hamir replied.

She looked up at him, eager to latch on to every word he said.

'I don't know the name or unit though. Tell me, did he wear a taweez?'

'Yes, for sure. Most Muslims wear a taweez. He wore one around his arm,' she replied.

'Did he have an account in the Bank of Pakistan?' Hamir queried.

'Yes, sir, Lahore branch.'

'Does 17, The Mall, Lahore mean anything to you?'

She went silent. He could see tears building up in her eyes.

'The address on the officer's chequebook was 17, The Mall, Lahore. We could also make out that the owner had signed a cheque on 2 December. The amount was quite large, I think it was for a sum of...'

Tears were now streaming down her cheeks as she opened her purse, slowly unfolding a cheque which she handed over to Hamir. It was the very same cheque, a cheque for Rs 2,000/-.

They sat in silence allowing the lady to regain her composure. After some time she spoke up.

'Tell me, sir. Were his last rights and burial done as per Islamic traditions?'

'Yes,' Hamir replied. 'He was given a befitting farewell. A farewell in the most honourable manner possible under the circumstances. His grave is also marked with a gravestone and is located on the banks of Drungali Nallah in the vicinity of Gurdwara Nangali close to Poonch.'

Hamir's assertion that her husband had been laid to rest in a proper manner had a calming effect on the lady. It had probably provided her the closure that she had been looking for. She thanked Hamir and left the room with her delightful daughter trotting behind.

Hamir never met the lady again. However, her cousin brother Major Hameed would visit him now and then. Whenever he came calling he would bring eatables which were always welcome. He had no doubt in his mind that Hameed's sister was the reason for his sporadic visits. For the widow Hamir was somehow the last link to her dead husband.

~

Hamir was beset with boredom and loneliness. In an attempt to keep himself engaged he had tried everything from sketching to even singing.

He would practise writing with his left hand given the limited mobility his right hand allowed. Every day he would spend some time replicating the text from magazines into his personal diary. The photos and advertisements contained in the magazines also provided the subject for sketching. His handwriting became better and his sketches reasonably good.

Singing of course was more challenging. The only music available to him was through the radio. For some reason the most played songs by Radio Pakistan at the time were of the famous ghazal singer Runa Laila.[32] Hamir had never tried singing before and to attempt to sing Runa Laila's ghazals would be ambitious to say the least. He didn't even try. He restricted himself to singing popular Indian film songs which he could recall from memory.

It had been some time since his last medical review. The surgical specialist had been very satisfied with his recovery after the operation and the resultant improvement in mobility of his hand. However, since his wrist had not fully regained its strength Hamir was prescribed physiotherapy.

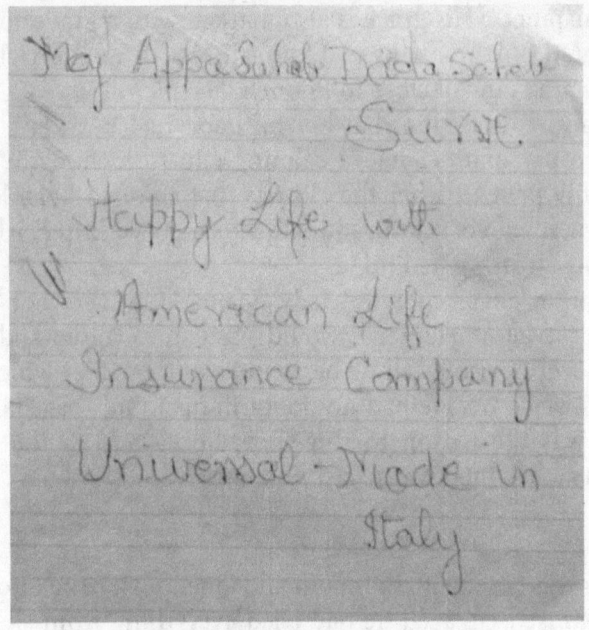

*Practising writing with his left hand.
On the top of the page is the name of his fellow inmate,
Major Surve; below it random words from
newspaper advertisements.*

Sketch made with heavily-bandaged right hand. Despite the limited mobility in this hand making writing rather strenuous, Hamir managed some stunning sketches following doctors' advice on exercising the right hand to aid recovery.

The Road to Recovery

During his stay at the hospital one of the things Hamir noticed was that the doctors were generally friendly, sincere and professional. They had no bias against treating Indians. However, the same could not be said of the non-commissioned officers (NCOs) some of whom seemed to nurse a grudge. Unfortunately the NCO responsible for Hamir's physiotherapy was one such individual.

Initially regular, as time passed the NCO became careless and insincere. He would just go through the motions, marking time, until the prescribed duration for physiotherapy was over. His visits became irregular and he would find the smallest of excuses to be absent. As a result the physiotherapy had little effect and Hamir's grip showed no improvement.

In sharp contrast the nursing staff, both male and female, were diligent, professional and caring, representing the best ethics of the medical profession.

The lowest rung of the hierarchy such as housekeepers, washermen, orderlies, barbers, etc., were simple people with no malice or prejudice at all. In their company Hamir would even forget that he was amidst Pakistanis. They were always warm and friendly. It was fun spending time with them. They provided him the entertainment and laughter he so longed for. If not for them his stay at the hospital would have been extremely boring and monotonous.

The surgical specialist carried out Hamir's next review sometime in late June. While all seemed well he was disappointed to find hardly any improvement in his grip. He prescribed a new regime of physiotherapy for the next four weeks.

Hamir didn't have it in his heart to tell him that the fault lay in the attitude of the NCO in charge and, therefore, the additional four weeks was unlikely to make a difference. He decided that it was best to seek permission to be discharged from the hospital.

During the next visit of the representative of the ICRC, in the presence of the commandant, Hamir made an impassioned plea to be discharged. He requested to be sent to the POW camp to join his fellow Indians as staying alone was becoming detrimental to his mental well-being.

Taking advantage of the presence of the commandant he requested that he may be discharged since he was the only Indian in the hospital. His continued presence was a needless security headache and administrative burden for the CMH, especially since no further medical treatment was required. He promised to undertake the physiotherapy exercises himself and that he would report for medical review whenever ordered. What Hamir said made sense to the commandant. He seemed to have been convinced though he avoided giving an immediate decision.

The person who broke the news of Hamir's departure from Rawalpindi was once again the barber. It was the morning of the first of July.

'Saabji, you are leaving today!' he said.

'Where to?' Hamir inquired.

'I heard they are shifting you today, sir.'

'Oh, OK. Shift? That means I will remain Pakistan's guest, right?' Hamir remarked, smiling. Later in the day he was informed that he would be leaving CMH, Rawalpindi in the evening. The barber returned to his room at lunchtime to bid him farewell.

'Sahab, it was a pleasure knowing a brave officer like you. It was a pleasure serving you,' he said, sounding somewhat emotional.

'Thank you very much. Spending time with you was fun,' Hamir replied.

'I wonder why our countries can't stop fighting! If only Indira Gandhi hadn't stopped the war early. A few more days and you would have captured the whole country and we would be together again!' the barber remarked.

What the barber said that night was a reflection of the demoralized state the Pakistanis found themselves in. Frustrated by the pettiness of their politicians and embarrassed by the surrender of their army there was a fair degree of anger against both politicians as well as the army. Hamir had often come across the disillusionment that the Pakistanis felt at that time.

In a few minutes the next visitor came across to bid him farewell. It was the 'safaiwala' who was responsible for cleaning his room. Hamir recognized him immediately. Hamir had spoken to him on a few occasions. He seemed to have an interest in the magazines Hamir received in the ICRC parcels. He had observed the man looking closely at the magazines on more than one occasion. He approached Hamir and said, 'Sahab, mujhe behad khushi hai aap apne watan wapas ja rahe hain, Khuda hafiz!' *I am very happy that you are returning to your country, Khuda hafiz!*

'Dhanyavad, haan, mujhe bhi,' Hamir replied. *Thank you. I am happy too.*

'Aapse ek darkhast hai, hazoor,' he said, a bit self-consciously.

'Haan, zaroor, bolo.'

'Sahab, kya main *Kalyan* magazine le sakta hoon?' he requested, picking up the magazine lying on his bedside. *Can I take your copy of the* Kalyan *magazine?* He spoke very softly, as if he didn't want anyone else to hear their conversation. 'Agar aap inhe wapas apne watan nahin le ja rahe?' *That is, if you aren't taking them back to your country.*

The Hindu prisoners in CMH would often receive a copy of the *Kalyan* magazine in their gift parcels. The monthly magazine printed at the Gita Press, Gorakhpur was essentially a spiritual magazine which carried religious and mythology-themed articles. While Hamir had never read the magazine in India, given the dearth of reading material he now read the all volumes he received. They made for interesting reading and provided a good perspective of the Hindu religion and mythology. No wonder the magazine had a dedicated band of followers back in India, he thought.

When Hamir saw the large photo of the saint Valmiki on the cover of the magazine that the man had picked, he immediately realized why it had caught his interest. Valmiki is thought to be the first Sanskrit poet and author of the holy

Hindu epic *Ramayana*. A cluster of marginalized communities in India have united to form the Valmiki community, claiming a common origin from this revered saint.

'Bilkul, main inhe yahin, almari main chhod jaunga. Jab hum chale jayein toh tum yahan se nikal lena,' Hamir suggested. *Absolutely, I will leave them in the cupboard. You can take them after I leave.* Hamir was pleasantly surprised by the underlying similarities and invisible threads that bound the two adversarial nations together, despite the many years since Partition.

In the afternoon a couple of attendants arrived at his room to help him pack. After his packing was done Hamir was blindfolded and led outside. He was assisted onto the rear of a large lorry in which a bed had been placed. As he lay down on the bed he could sense the presence of a few guards around him.

The flurry of activity had been observed by Hamir's other friend—the generator operator, who was standing near the vehicle. 'Sahabji, tussi ja rahe ho?' he said in Punjabi. *Sir, you are leaving?*

'Haan, miyan, aspatal chhod raha hoon, magar abhi Pakistan mein hi rahunga!' Hamir replied. *Yes, leaving the hospital. But I will remain in Pakistan yet!*

'Ab kahan milenge, sahabji. Menu yaad rakhna! Khuda hafiz,' he added. *I don't think we will meet again, sir. Do remember me.* The humble generator operator sounded emotional too.

'Thank you very much, miyan. I will never forget the days I spent here. Khuda hafiz,' Hamir said. He hadn't realized the number of friends he had made at Rawalpindi.

As the lorry left CMH in the late afternoon Hamir's mind was beset with several questions. *Was it the last he was seeing of the hospital? Had he made the right decision to volunteer for the prisoner of war camp? Would he be as comfortable as he was in the hospital?*

The uncertainty of his immediate future made him slightly anxious and as the vehicle carrying him settled to a steady pace he weighed all possible future scenarios. Amid all this the sentimental import of leaving Rawalpindi was relegated to the background and he missed the significance of his final departure from the hospital. It wasn't long before sleep got the better of him.

Part Three

POW CAMP, LYALLPUR

1 July 1972. Rawalpindi–Lyallpur Road

Da dump...da dump...da dump...

The dull and repetitive sound startled Hamir out of his sleep. Blindfolded and disoriented, he had no idea where he was. The air felt damp. They were close to a large water body.

'Sahab, dekho! Hamari Jhelum. Kabhi aapne itna bada pul dekha hai?' one of the sentries shouted to be heard above the noise of the engine. *Sahab, look! It's our Jhelum. Have you ever seen such a huge bridge?*

So that explains the sound and smell, Hamir thought. *If we are on the Jhelum Bridge we must be heading south.*

'I have seen many large bridges but I can't see your Jhelum. I am blindfolded, remember?' Hamir mocked. The guards had decided to halt a while near the bridge for a cup of tea.

Hamir's hands were handcuffed to the body of the vehicle giving the guard reasonable confidence that he couldn't escape. To Hamir's relief his blindfold was removed.

It was late evening and the Jhelum River looked splendid against the setting sun. He enjoyed the beautiful sunset while sipping his tea. In the moment he had even forgotten that he was a POW, until his guard blindfolded him again. However, the blindfold didn't bother Hamir any more. It had become dark and sitting inside the cargo area of the truck he couldn't see anything anyway.

The journey for the next couple of hours was uneventful. Bored, Hamir found himself drifting in and out of sleep.

Late at night their vehicle came to a halt at the main gate of Lyallpur[33] Central Jail. Opening the heavy iron gates at night was a rather cumbersome task and it created quite a cacophony which woke Hamir up.

He was escorted to a small room where his blindfold was

removed and he was offered a cup of tea while he waited for the formalities to be completed.

Lyallpur Jail was built in 1967 by President Ayub Khan. It was constructed with a view to confining long-term prisoners of the region. In the recent past in addition to criminals it had housed political dissidents as well.

Initially most Indian prisoners were lodged in civilian prisons close to where they had been captured. In early 1971 a decision was taken to place all POWs in the Lyallpur Central Jail for administrative convenience.

Built as a high-security jail the prison at Lyallpur was quite formidable. It had three rings of ten-feet-high walls, electrified barbed wire and watchtowers manned by guards armed with machine guns.[34] At night the area would be flooded with searchlights. While there was no compromise from the security point of view, comfort was accorded much lower priority. The accommodation for the prisoners was very basic.

With Hamir moving to Lyallpur he would be the seniormost POW among the seven army officers and 600 men of other ranks residing in the jail. Since the prison had been designed for a capacity of over 1,200 availability of adequate space was perhaps the only silver lining.

By the time Hamir was escorted to his cell it was nearing dawn. The cell consisted of a walled courtyard not more than six feet by six feet. The courtyard had an open roof enclosed with a cage-like structure to prevent escape. The morning sky was visible through the cage-like structure.

Adjoining the courtyard was a very small room in which a cement plinth served as a bed. An Indian-style squat toilet was the only other 'convenience' provided in the room, though the chain for activating the flush was located outside the cell. This meant that the guard would need to be requested to pull the chain whenever a flush was required. Thankfully the water tap next to the squat toilet had running water. A small dirty plastic mug had been placed below the tap.

The cell hadn't been cleaned for quite some time and was filthy. The plinth on which he was expected to sleep had layers of dust on it and would need cleaning if he was to lie on it even for a moment.

From among his belongings Hamir took out the turban cloth which he had fondly kept all these months. Using the plastic mug he flooded the cement plinth with water and with the turban cloth he wiped the dust off the cement plinth. After about an hour of hard work he finally had a reasonably clean cell and a passable bed to sleep on. But there was no point sleeping as it was morning now and the camp had begun to come to life.

Hamir washed up and waited for his morning tea, which was delivered to him at five-thirty. It was now time for his morning ablutions.

At the hospital Hamir had the luxury of a personal barber. In Lyallpur he would have to shave on his own. Luckily for him one of the parcels he had received at Lyallpur contained a brand new shaving kit. Hamir was seriously out of practice and shaving was quite an effort. There was no mirror, the light was poor and to make matters worse his bandaged right hand impeded movement. It took him a long time to finish. But by the time breakfast arrived he was reasonably presentable, except for the few nicks that he had managed to obtain in the process.

Breakfast consisted of a couple of parathas and some vegetables, all placed together in a steel thali which was slid into his cell through a gap below the iron door. This gap had been deliberate, to allow the meals to be shoved through without the requirement of opening the door. Meals were prepared by Indian prisoners and the food delivered to each officer under the supervision of a Pakistani guard. Though a change from the English breakfast he was accustomed to at Rawalpindi, the Indian-style breakfast tasted fine.

Later that morning an officer came visiting. He was broadly built, middle-aged and wore civvies.

'You are Hamir Singh?' he asked.

'Yes, that's right,' Hamir replied.

'Welcome to Lyallpur Central Jail.'

'Thank you, sir.'

'I hope you're comfortable?'

'Yes, sir, very comfortable thank you,' Hamir answered, with a hint of sarcasm which the officer ignored.

The officer glanced around Hamir's cell, closely observing his kit. He noticed that some items of the prisoner's kit were missing.

'Sahab, where's the mattress and blanket?' he asked the JCO accompanying him.

'Major sahab has just arrived, sir. We have only issued him some of the kit. The quartermaster will hand over all the balance items shortly,' the JCO replied.

'OK, give me the completion report when it's done, right?'

'Ji huzoor.'

'OK, Major, you settle down, take some rest. The journey must have tired you out. I'll catch you later,' the officer suggested as he left the cell.

'Roger, sir,' Hamir acknowledged.

With nothing better to do, Hamir lay down on the bed. *What next*, he wondered. *Will I spend the remainder of my time in solitary confinement in this miserable place?*

At midday he was served lunch which consisted of a small quantity of watery dal, mixed vegetable and some chapatis. Though average in taste the flavours were Indian and it was a nice change.

The hot July sun and the high humidity made him sweaty and miserable. By late afternoon his cell felt like a pressure cooker. He tried moving outside but the courtyard provided no respite as the sun beat through its open roof. The only option was to wipe away the sweat streaming down his face. He kept at it, wiping his face every now and then until late evening when the temperature became bearable and his sweating finally stopped.

There was no way he was going to spend the night cooped up in the small room which by evening had become dark and claustrophobic. He went out of the room. It was slightly better outside as the ventilation allowed a gentle breeze. Sleeping

POW Camp, Lyallpur

outside would definitely be a better option.

He found himself a flat piece of ground where he spread his bed sheet. Satisfied, he lay down to sleep.

He tossed and turned, trying his best to find some sleep but to no avail. Swarms of hungry mosquitoes descended on him with a vengeance.

Although Hamir covered himself from head to toe with a damp cloth the irritating sound of the mosquitoes allowed him no peace. He remained sleepless, staring at the sky and stars.

Bored, with nothing better to do, he started humming a song. Somehow that made him feel better, which suggested to him the idea of singing himself to sleep.

'Jaane kahan gaye woh din...' Hamir's voice reverberated in the courtyard. *Where have those days gone...* The lyrics of the Raj Kapoor classic sounded particularly poignant given his present circumstances.

All this while the guard outside his cell had been observing Hamir closely, amused by his decision to sing late at night and the apt lyrics of the songs.

The next day the Pakistani officer who had welcomed Hamir to Lyallpur visited him again. This time he wore his uniform, allowing Hamir to read his name. He was Major Khwaja the deputy camp commandant of Lyallpur POW camp. On meeting Hamir he asked him whether he had received all of his kit.

'I hope you received your mattress and blanket,' Khwaja inquired.

'No,' Hamir replied.

Khwaja turned to the JCO accompanying him and shouted angrily—'Kyun, sahab? Abhi tak Major sahab ko mattress aur blanket kyun nahin di gayi?' *Why, sahab? Why hasn't he been given the mattress and blanket?* The JCO had no answer.

'Aap apni tashreef le ja sakte hain!' he said sarcastically. 'Adhe ghante mein sab issue ho jaana chahiye, samjhe?' *Get out! The stuff must be issued in the next half an hour, you understand?*

'Sorry for that. Do you need anything else?'

'No, I'm fine, thank you,' Hamir said.

'Good, then see you later.' Khwaja left the cell.

On his way out Khwaja chose to interact with Hamir's sentry and sitting in his cell Hamir could eavesdrop on their conversation.

'How did Major sahab spend his night?' Major Khwaja queried.

'Nothing at all, sahabji. He spent the entire night singing songs.'

'Arre, kya baat kar rahe ho? Gaana ga rahe the!' Khwaja exclaimed, irritated. *What are you saying? Singing songs, my foot!*

'Allah kasam, sahab! Gaate hi ja rahe the!' the poor man insisted. *By God, sir! He just kept singing!*

Hamir was amused. His singing had at least kept his guard awake too! Khwaja left the area muttering to himself; clearly he wasn't amused.

The morning had started well. An early morning drizzle had made it relatively pleasant. Hamir decided to get some fresh air. The moment he stepped out of his cell he heard someone yell—'Don't worry, everything will be fine. Just be patient for a few days!'

He couldn't actually see the person as his view was blocked by the high walls of the courtyard. The person continued—'You will be fine! This is just normal procedure!'

The man's voice came from the direction of a double-storey barrack about 100 yards away. From Hamir's courtyard only its roof was visible.

'Suno, miyan!' Hamir called out to his guard. *Listen!*

'Yes, sahab, what is it?' the guard replied.

'Tell me, who is this person shouting? What is he saying?' Hamir inquired.

'Arre, sahab, it's one of your soldiers. He is just trying to keep your morale high.'

Hamir would learn later that what he was being subjected to was the usual welcome one got at Lyallpur. After two to three days of solitary confinement they would normally be shifted with other prisoners.

Fellow prisoners had probably got to know that a new prisoner had arrived at Lyallpur Central Jail. They were trying to lift his spirits to make it easier for him during his solitary confinement. Hamir though was far from demoralized.

~

A few days later the camp commandant Lieutenant Colonel Mohammad Latif Malik visited Hamir.

'Hello, Major, I am Colonel Malik. How are you?'

'Hello, sir. I am perfectly alright,' Hamir replied.

'You are the one from 14 Grenadiers, isn't it?' Malik asked.

'Yes, sir, that's correct.'

'We have some of your men here at Lyallpur too. They want to meet you,' Malik informed him.

'Really, sir? I would love to meet them, if you permit,' Hamir requested.

'You know, Major, today is Friday.'

'I am afraid I don't know that, sir, I have no idea what day it is!' Hamir really had no idea.

'Being a Friday, we have the Jummah namaz at 1 PM,' Malik continued. 'Your men insist you should join them.'

Hamir in the small but lovingly decorated unit masjid, before the war.

Hamir smiled. The men of Charlie Company must have learnt that he had reached Lyallpur. As their company commander, Hamir usually joined their Friday prayers. If they knew he was present at Lyallpur they would expect him to join the Jummah namaz.

'Would you like to join them?' Malik inquired.

'Yes, of course!' Hamir replied.

'Are you quite sure?'

'Absolutely, sir, why do you ask?'

'Because you are a Hindu?' Malik remarked.

'Sir, for my company I am a Muslim,' Hamir replied. 'It's a tradition in our army. Every company commander follows the religion of his command. I command Muslim men and it's my duty to join them for namaz.'

'Really! This I got to see!' he said in disbelief.

'You will only be able to if you allow me to join my men.'

'OK, let me see what I can do.'

Malik left the room looking pretty amused. At about twenty past twelve another officer, Major Sher Jaman, arrived at Hamir's cell.

'I believe you want to join the Jummah namaz,' he remarked.

'Yes, that's correct.'

'OK. Then come with me.'

Hamir accompanied the major to the mosque which was within the jail premises. As they arrived at the mosque Hamir removed his shoes and headed in the direction of the water tank. He washed his face, hands, elbows, head and his feet, right up to his ankles. He then rinsed his mouth.

From a distance, out of Hamir's view, a group of inquisitive officers were keenly observing the Indian Hindu company commander.

As the call for prayer was announced Hamir joined in like any devout Muslim, bowing and prostrating himself, immaculately following the rules of prayer. To any bystander he would appear a regular Muslim.

Colonel Malik, and Majors Khwaja and Sher Jaman watched amazed. For them it was an unbelievable spectacle.

As soon as the prayer finished Hamir's men rushed to meet him. They were delighted to see him alive and crowded around him excitedly.

His men had last seen him grappling bare-handed with the enemy. Since he wasn't with them at the POW camp they had assumed he had died in battle. Though they had heard rumours that Hamir had arrived at Lyallpur they refused to believe them until they saw him with their own eyes.

There was lots of excited conversation; Hamir had much catching up to do. He was keen to know what had transpired after his capture. As a result, although the prayers had finished quite some time back the men stood chatting with their company commander. Sher Jaman, who allowed the conversation, waited patiently, watching them closely. Finally, as it was getting late he decided to intervene. He walked up to Hamir and politely requested him to return to his cell.

The Pakistani officers' respect for Hamir grew considerably consequent to what they had seen during the Jummah namaz. As they left the mosque Hamir was guided to a new cell in the section of the prison where all the other officers were housed.

Hamir's solitary confinement at Lyallpur Central Jail ended on 7 July 1972.

~

As Hamir arrived at the army officers' enclosure he found six officers waiting for him. They wore the standard POW clothing—a grey shirt and a matching salwar of the same colour.

Before Hamir, Captain Fardun Dastoor was the seniormost among the six POWs housed at Lyallpur. The other five were Captain Anil Athale (the next seniormost), Lieutenant Ganga Ram Chaudhary, Captain Mehrotra, Lieutenant A.G.J. Sweetens and Lieutenant Vijender Singh Gurung.

The officers introduced themselves to Hamir. He hadn't known the officers earlier. Most of them had earned their commission when Hamir was in Nigeria. The only officer he had met earlier was Ganga Ram Chaudhary, whom he had met at CMH, Rawalpindi.

While they met Hamir noticed that a white cross had been marked on the back of every prisoner's shirt. He was informed that the sole purpose of this was to help in aiming at a prisoner attempting to escape.

The Indian POWs were kept at four different locations in the prison. The army officers were kept in a separate section which consisted of a large barrack partitioned into seven parts for the officers. A second section consisted of four double-storey barracks in which all soldiers, except Muslims, were housed. Each double-storey barrack had approximately 140 soldiers living in them. The third section consisted of approximately forty Muslim soldiers who were kept away from men of other religions.

The stated Pakistani reason for this was their special dietary preferences and need for prayer. The more plausible reason, however, was that it would facilitate attempts to indoctrinate them.

The air force officers' block was located approximately 100 yards away from the army officers' block. It consisted of two long barracks, one behind the other and a patch of open space in between. Each barrack was further partitioned into several separate cells, exactly similar in design to the one where Hamir had been lodged while in solitary confinement at Lyallpur.

The entire block was enclosed by a perimeter wall. There was only a single gate to enter the enclosed area of each block. This was always kept locked. Since the single gate and perimeter walls provided adequate security the doors of individual cells were left open by day.

The prisoners were free to intermingle within the confines of the enclosed portion of each block. This was welcome as officers could spend time talking to each other during the morning hours.

Since there were fewer officers than cells available in each enclosure, vacant cells were utilized as baths or toilets. Some of the vacant cells were also occupied by fellow Indian soldiers who were nominated to help in administration.

Though squat toilets were available in each cell, officers used only the squat toilets of the vacant cells at the extremity of each barrack.

The space between the barracks was used for activities such as badminton or volleyball. A part of the area was also converted into a kitchen garden.

Keeping an eagle eye on them were armed guards perched high on specially constructed watch towers overlooking the entire block. At night searchlights would flood the entire complex.

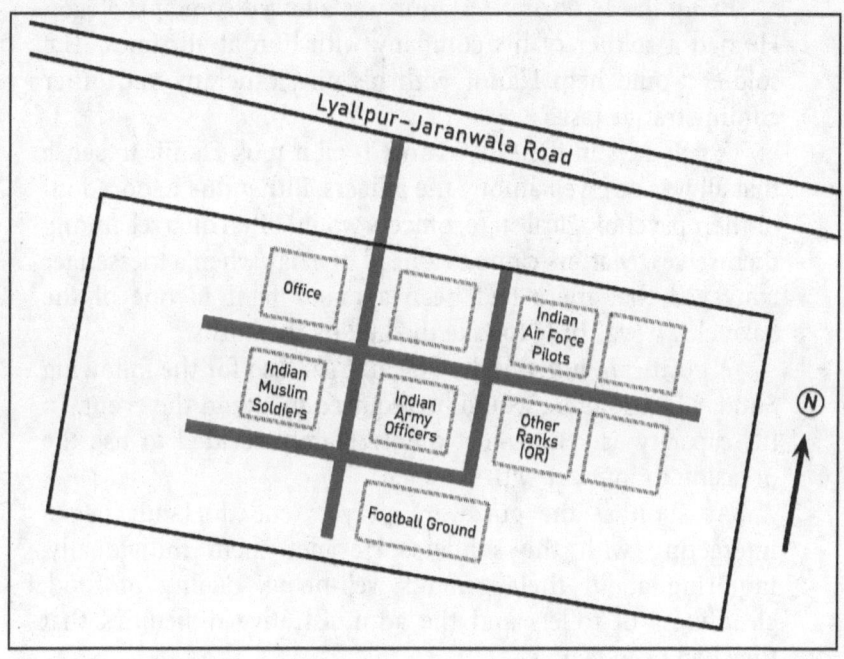

Rough layout of the Lyallpur Jail.[35] (Not to scale.)

Other than the living areas the POWs were permitted to carry out physical activity of limited duration within their respective enclosures.

There was a mosque on campus for the Muslim POWs to offer their prayers. The POWs were provided newspapers and magazines to read.

Communication between Indian POWs located in separate enclosures was clandestinely carried out by the soldiers who were tasked to deliver food. They were very suitable for courier duties as they were allowed access to all sections of the prison complex.

Being the seniormost Hamir was allowed some privileges. He had a soldier of his company with him at all times. The soldier would help Hamir with his physiotherapy and other administrative tasks.

A few days in the POW camp is all it took Hamir to sense that all was not well among the officers. Either due to boredom or their psychological state, officers would often quarrel among themselves. Matters came to a head one day when a messenger conveyed that there had been a major fight in one of the barracks. It was time to take the bull by the horns.

A gurdwara function had been organized for the following Sunday. All soldiers would be required to attend the event. In his capacity as seniormost officer Hamir decided to use the occasion to interact with the men.

As soon as the gurdwara prayers ended Hamir began interacting with the soldiers. He met them individually, inquiring about their general well-being, quality of food, cleanliness of toilets and the administrative difficulties that they had been facing.

The sense he got from the interaction was that the main issue was lack of physical activity. Except for thirty-odd minutes of perfunctory PT, they were not allowed to play football, volleyball or engage in any other recreational exercise. To make matters worse there was just one volleyball court, hence only very few men got the opportunity to play.

Major Khwaja, who was on duty, had been watching while

Hamir interacted with the men. The post-prayer interaction had almost turned into a Sainik Sammelan. He seemed worried with what Hamir was doing.

'Major Hamir, it's time for the men to return to their barracks,' Khwaja remarked.

'Please wait, Major, I need some more time. I need to know how they are!' Hamir replied.

'Their well-being is our responsibility, please don't worry! As it is you've had enough time,' he added impatiently.

'Major Khwaja, I am sure you are aware of the Geneva Conventions. If not, I suggest you take a look at them. As the seniormost Indian officer here I am entitled to seek the welfare of the POWs!' Hamir didn't really know whether there was any such provision in the Geneva Conventions but his confidence convinced Khwaja that he was probably right.

'Major, you don't need to teach me about the Geneva Conventions,' said Khwaja curtly.

'Then how is it that you are not allowing us adequate exercise?' Hamir asked.

'Of course we are allowing that! Don't you have PT every morning?'

'PT? For your information it's just thirty minutes of lollygagging!' Hamir had turned combative. 'Why don't you allow us to play football? Why aren't there adequate volleyball courts? Do you think one court is enough for 600 soldiers?'

'We can't allow gathering in large numbers, it's a security issue!' Khwaja replied.

'Security, my foot! You are just denying us our rights. If you can't handle us please take me to the Camp Commandant. I would like an audience with him!' Hamir was livid.

'OK. If that's what you want I will convey it to him. But please ask your men to disperse. I have had enough of this,' Khwaja declared.

Meanwhile, observing the heated argument, an alert had been sounded. All guards were at stand-to, aiming their weapons aggressively towards the POWs gathered there. Hamir realized that it was time to step back from the confrontation. He had achieved the desired effect.

The Indian soldiers had witnessed the argument too. As they dispersed they seemed happy that someone had finally taken up cudgels on their behalf.

'Ab humare Major sahab ne sambhal liya hai. Kuch na kuch achha nateeja to niklega!' they said. *Now that our Major has taken charge there will be a positive outcome for sure!*

The very next day Hamir was summoned to the camp commandant's office. As soon as he entered, Lieutenant Colonel Malik, who had been busy studying files, looked up and greeted him.

'Good morning, Hamir. I believe you have some issues,' he said sternly.

'Good morning, sir. Yes, you are right. I do have some *issues*. Kindly give me a patient hearing,' Hamir replied.

'Go ahead, Major, tell me,' Malik was all ears.

'Sir, all I ask is what constitutes our rights as per the Geneva Conventions.'

'OK, go on.'

'Sir, my men aren't getting adequate exercise. With the limited exercise they seem restless. We need to be allowed to play football and volleyball,' Hamir pleaded. 'There aren't adequate volleyball courts. It would be wonderful if we could have one in each block. We will prepare the fields, we just need the equipment.'

'OK, I will try,' Malik replied.

'Great, sir. If we have adequate fields then we will like to conduct inter-block matches. That will lighten up the atmosphere... And, sir, I have another request.'

'And what's that?' Malik said, exasperated.

'I am told we have only a gurdwara function every Sunday. Why not a mandir function?'

'The mandir function is organized once a month,' Malik said.

'Sir, I would like to request you to organize mandir and gurdwara functions on alternate Sundays. All of us will attend both these events irrespective of our religion.'

'That shouldn't be a problem, I will see to it.'

'And my final request, sir...' Hamir was stretching his luck now.

'Achha bhai, go ahead, yeh bhi bata do!' Malik smiled. *Go ahead, might as well tell me that too!*

'Sir, we would like our Muslim boys to live with us. In the Indian Army we don't believe in divisions based on religion or caste.'

'See, Hamir, this is something I can't promise. It's beyond me. Orders are from higher HQ. I will try, but no promises,' Malik replied, sounding embarrassed.

'I am sure if you try hard enough you will succeed, sir.' Now Hamir was smiling. Malik laughed loudly. When Hamir left the commandant's office he was reasonably confident that his requests would be accepted.

Malik was true to his word. Except the request to shift the Muslim soldiers all other requests were met. Hamir shared the good news with the soldiers after the mandir parade the next Sunday morning. They were delighted; finally some of their long-standing demands had been met.

The men spent the next few days and weeks preparing fields and organizing teams. Contestants began practising seriously for the forthcoming inter-block football and volleyball tournaments.

To Hamir's relief quarrels and petty arguments became rare as the men expended all their energy and angst on the sports field.

An avid sportsman, Hamir himself became a regular on the field. The atmosphere in the camp became better now that there was something for every soldier to look forward to, either as a spectator, cheerleader or player.

~

'Gentlemen, I have an announcement. Please lend me your ears!' Hamir called out.

The officers were playing bridge under the tree in two groups. They looked towards Hamir, surprised.

'Go ahead, sir, we are listening,' Gurung yelled back.

'Good news, we will be home in December. Back to India!' Hamir announced.

Earlier in the morning the POWs had received mail. Hamir was delighted to receive his first letter. He recognized the handwriting; it was from Laxmi. He grabbed the letter and rushed to his cell in excitement. He needed to read the letter in private.

Laxmi's letter was reasonably long. Always expressive, she had lots to share with Hamir and wouldn't like to miss out any piece of information. But though the page had been filled in the smallest handwriting possible, it had been done so fairly neatly.

She wrote that Kanwarsa had been posted to Dholpur since February as part of the anti-dacoity operations in the Chambal Valley.[36] She worried for him as he was involved in daily operations either searching for dacoits or getting them to surrender.

The children had joined a local school at Dholpur. Kanwarsa had recently bought a car and the kids had been super excited. It was a vintage emerald green Packard[37] which was earlier part of the Raja of Dholpur's personal collection. The kids would spend the evening either cycling or taking a joy ride in the majestic vehicle.

Vijay had picked up quite a bit of Hindi, while Vikram had gained height. Lalita and Saroj—Laxmi's younger sisters— had been busy organizing variety entertainment programmes for the family. They had even been able to make Vijay dance for them, which was quite an achievement. The kids missed their father and so did she. Vijay insisted that he would write something for Hamir and she was allowing him space for that. He had drawn a smiling face near the bottom of the page. Below that was scribbled in English—'*My papa will come home in December.*'

'So, gentlemen, as I said, we will be home in December. My son says so in this letter,' Hamir burst out laughing as he held up the letter and waved it in the air.

~

The inter-block football championship commenced. The football field was ready and spectators took their places on the sidelines. Since almost all the POWs had arrived to watch the match a large presence of guards had also been ensured. Major Sher Jaman was the duty officer and he sat on his chair waiting for the match to start.

Of the three Pakistani officers Major Sher Jaman was the friendliest. A Pathan from Karachi, Jaman would often join their company. The Indian officers became fond of him as well. He was their go-to man whenever they needed to approach the authorities with a request.

Each soldier was issued two sets of grey POW uniforms. The officers, based on a recent request, were now allowed khaki uniforms to distinguish them from the others. Other than these basic clothes there was nothing else to wear. For the tournament they needed appropriate clothes.

Fortunately some of the Gorkha soldiers had a basic knowledge of cutting and stitching cloth. All cloth received through the International Red Cross was collected. Cloth of any type would do. Bed sheets, pillow covers and turban cloth were sought after, as were the Gorkha soldiers, who would expertly do the cutting. Other soldiers with basic hand-sewing skills were tasked to stitch the cut cloth together into shorts and shirts. Before long a set of sportswear was available for the players.

The result of the enterprise was that these soldiers acquired a special status of sorts and the demand for private clothing soared.

Many fortunate prisoners started flaunting colourful clothes and night suits. Shirts made of turban cloth were especially popular as the cloth material was breathable and comfortable in the hot and humid conditions of Lyallpur. As a result Sikh soldiers found a host of fair-weather friends in their quest for turban cloth. The less fortunate had to make do with the next best option—bed sheets or tablecloth.

The match was between Block A and Block B.

Block A consisted of Gorkha soldiers, considered good at football.

Soldiers belonging to the Grenadiers regiment represented Block B. Though not particularly good at football they were renowned for their stamina and 'josh'—zeal. Their expertise, however, was generally restricted to cross-country, volleyball or kabaddi.

Since officers and JCOs were not part of any particular block their teams were decided by a draw of lots. Gurung was on the ground waiting for the draw of lots the result of which decided that he was to play for the Gorkha block.

At precisely 06:00 hours the match referee blew his whistle announcing the commencement of the match.

A good player, Gurung's speed and excellent ball control made him an ideal right out. A combination of his speedy forays and the Gorkhas' ball skills was too much for the opposing team. By halftime Gurung's team had a comfortable 3-0 lead.

At halftime Block B revised their strategy. Gurung had to be reined in and Sepoy Shaukat, a huge hulk of a soldier, was assigned this special mission. Basically a pehelwan, he had never tried his luck at football. Team B believed that Shaukat's bulk would be good enough to block Gurung.

As soon as the second half commenced Team B was horrified at Shaukat's leisurely movements on the field. He just couldn't get the hang of the game and was found to be failing miserably in trying to restrain Gurung. Another accurate pass by him resulted in the fourth goal.

Exasperated, the team captain made Shaukat the target of his anger as he hurled a verbal volley of expletives at him. The abuses seemed to have a magical effect on Shaukat. When Gurung came running down the right flank the next time Shaukat timed his movement to perfection and rammed his head into Gurung. Gurung's speed and Shaukat's momentum resulted in an ugly collision. You could hear a pin drop as players and spectators rushed to the injured players.

Shaukat had taken the collision well. He was soon back on his feet, shrugging his shoulders, wondering what the fuss was all about. Poor Gurung took quite a while to recover from the clash.

The remainder of the match was to most spectators an astonishing display of Gurung's grit. The match ended with a resounding victory for Team A. They had won 6-1. As the players shook hands and headed for refreshments Sher Jaman walked up to Gurung who was lovingly called 'Chhotu', and shook his hand.

'Chhotu, you sure are a talented player. Well played!'

~

The celebratory bada khana—feast—was going great guns. It was Saturday evening and the Gorkhas had won the tournament and it was time to let their hair down. With no supply of their beloved rum the men did the next best thing—they sang and danced.

Soon, Lieutenant Gurung aka Chhotu was shoved onto the stage and his soldiers demanded he sing a song. He began singing and his voice had a magical effect on the men. Happy and cheerful, they joined Chhotu Gurung, singing along loudly. Momentarily they had forgotten all their troubles. Hamir had never seen the men in better spirits.

Next morning Hamir walked up to Sher Jaman with a request. The fifteenth of August, the Indian Independence Day, was a few weeks away and on the eve of that occasion he proposed that the POWs host a variety entertainment programme for the camp officials and guards.

'Major, please consider our request,' Hamir pleaded. 'It will make a major difference to morale. Besides, it will reflect well on your authorities when the International Red Cross visit next,' he added.

'No promises, but it's worth a try. Let me have a word with the Camp Commandant,' Sher Jaman replied.

Major Sher Jaman had attended the previous evening's celebratory bada khana. Sportingly, on popular request, he had even joined the singing.

To permit a variety entertainment by the POWs on the eve of the Indian Independence Day was a pretty harmless request. Personally he agreed with Hamir entirely. It would be good for morale. The commandant could showcase the event by inviting the local senior officers. He was reasonably confident that he would get the permission.

August 1972

The news that a variety entertainment programme was being planned generated a buzz in the camp. There was a stream of visitors at the officers' barracks volunteering to take part in the programme.

The overall responsibility was given to Ganga Ram Chaudhary who took to the task with enthusiasm. He methodically organized the volunteers into various small teams.

One team was nominated to prepare the singers required for the programme. Chhotu Gurung, who was blessed with an excellent voice, volunteered to take on this task. The go-to man Major Sher Jaman was requested to arrange some musical instruments. Promptly a guitar and drum were made available. The harmonium and dholak from the mandir/gurdwara coupled with the guitar and drum set enabled the creation of a formidable musical opera. A few ghazals and popular qawwalis were planned for the occasion. The daily rehearsals filled the precincts of the camp with the melodious sound of music.

The second team was tasked to organize appropriate skits or dances for the occasion. This was taken on by the Gorkhas voluntarily. Though they had adequate volunteers they had to accommodate a few boys from the Grenadiers who were keen to showcase their wit through a specially produced ragini based on life in the POW camp. A popular part of any bada khana, their ragini had to be included. The icing on the cake was a bit of bhangra put up by the Sikh soldiers.

Decorations and appropriate dresses for the event were handled by the third team. All soldiers with stitching skills were enlisted for this task. All available cloth was collected and by the first week of August they had stitched together a colourful set of clothes appropriate for the event. Chhotu

Gurung designed caps for the qawwals which were stitched to perfection, lending authenticity to their performance.

The last team was responsible for looking after the construction of the stage and seating arrangements, which were very basic. Chairs were placed for all officers and security staff while the rest of the soldiers would sit on the ground.

After a few days of practice the prisoners were successful in putting together a grand entertainment programme. With just a day left everyone waited excitedly for the big event.

In the evening of the fourteenth of August as men started gathering for the event Major Sher Jaman seemed nervous. Large gatherings had never been allowed after dark before. The Pakistani guards were not taking any chances and were on alert. LMGs were sited and manned on all four corners of the camp. Beneath the thin veneer of amiability the stark reality of being a POW was never far.

Just as the programme was about to commence the camp commandant walked in followed by seven men escorted by guards.

'Hamir, have you met your guests?'

'My guests?' Hamir replied, puzzled. He wasn't expecting any guests.

'Meet your brother air force officers; they have just joined us from Rawalpindi,' Malik announced.

The officers introduced themselves one by one. They were Wing Commander B.A. Coelho, Squadron Leaders D.S. Jafa and Kamat, Flight Lieutenants Bhargava and Tejwant Singh, Flying Officers Chati and K.C. Kuruvilla.

Hamir later learnt that consequent to an attempt by three Indian Air Force officers to escape the POW camp at Rawalpindi all ten Indian Air Force officers lodged at Rawalpindi had been shifted to Lyallpur. Flight Lieutenants Dilip Parulkar, M.S. Grewal and Harish Sinhji, who had made the unsuccessful attempt, had been placed in solitary confinement.

The 'guests' were provided seats after which the camp commandant left the premises as the programme commenced.

Whatever tension there may have been earlier melted the

moment the programme began. Soon every spectator including the guards was totally engrossed, enjoying every minute of it.

Ganga Ram Chaudhary's melodious ghazals and Chhotu's peppy qawwalis filled the air. They could put any singer to shame. The skits and bhangra were big hits too. By the end of the evening every person witnessing the programme was well entertained. The event had gone off extremely well.

The report of the successful event reached the camp commandant. The next morning Hamir was summoned to his office.

'Good morning and Happy Independence Day,' Colonel Malik said.

'Good morning, sir. Thank you very much.'

'I believe you guys put together a wonderful show,' Malik remarked.

'I think it came out pretty well, sir.'

'Sher Jaman mentioned that it was a good programme. Can I ask you for a favour?' he asked.

'Sure, sir.'

'Could you repeat the programme for our men?'

'Sure, sir.'

'And a few officers and their families,' Malik added.

'No problem, sir. When would you like us to organize the programme?' Hamir inquired.

'That's your call, Major, you decide the date.'

Hamir thought for a while. Janmashtami, the festival celebrating the birth of Lord Krishna was due on 1 September. A programme in the evening would be fine as it would facilitate a mandir function at midnight, the traditional time of prayer. Malik didn't mind the idea.

'But, I have a request, sir,' Hamir stated.

'OK, what's that?'

'Sir, after the programme please allow us to offer our prayers in the mandir. Janmashtami prayers are offered at midnight.'

'OK, let me see what I can do. It may be a security issue. I will try though,' Malik promised.

'Thank you, sir.' Hamir was happy with what concessions he had been able to obtain.

They were later informed that permission for midnight prayers had been denied due to security concerns. However, they would be allowed to offer their prayers the next morning.

September 1972

A large gathering watched the entertainment programme at the POW camp, Lyallpur. As expected it was a smashing hit and received a thunderous applause from the Indian as well as Pakistani spectators.

The Janmashtami celebrations had some other positive spinoffs as well. Due to the bonhomie created by the event the air force officers were able to extract a promise from Malik to end the solitary confinement of their three colleagues.

The event also contributed to breaking the ice between the Indians and the camp authorities at Lyallpur. Relations improved and the atmosphere became friendly.

The weekly religious programmes at the mandir or gurdwara were well attended thereby providing enough volunteers to sing the bhajans. This resulted in a healthy competition wherein each tried to outdo the performance of the other. Bhajans and kirtans were rendered in a most professional manner.

By the end of September the days became shorter and the weather turned pleasant. The nights were cool and it was obvious that soon light blankets would be required.

While the officers and JCOs had been given a blanket each there were not enough blankets for all the soldiers. Hamir realized the same one day while interacting with the men. Lyallpur was likely to get extremely cold in winter. It was crucial that the issue be raised with the commandant as soon as possible.

October 1972

Despite his request Hamir was allowed a meeting with the commandant only in the evening of the third of October.

When he arrived a meeting was in progress. He was informed that he would be able to see Colonel Malik only after the meeting was over.

While he waited Hamir noticed that the office staff was unusually reserved and the atmosphere was tense.

It was close to five when the meeting concluded. As Hamir entered Colonel Malik's office, Major Khwaja and Sher Jaman were in the process of leaving. Both ignored Hamir when he wished them as they passed by. This was unusual. Normally they would nod in acknowledgment or at least offer a smile. Clearly something serious had happened.

'Yes, Major, what is it?' Malik asked.

'Sir, I have come to make a request on behalf of the men,' Hamir replied.

'OK, what's it now?'

Hamir then went on to present his case, highlighting the need for every man to be provided a blanket as soon as possible in view of the fast approaching winter. Malik's response was lukewarm.

'I will do my best, Major,' he concluded, getting up, ready to leave.

'Sir, I hope it's done soon enough. The men were kind of protesting!' Hamir commented.

'Protesting? Please don't encourage the use of this word! It will anger my men. Although we are not murderers. This is Rawalpindi, not Dhana!'[38] he remarked, sounding angry.

Hamir was puzzled. He had no idea what had triggered Malik's anger. *Why was he talking about Dhana?*

'Beg your pardon, sir, I didn't understand!' Hamir replied, confused.

'Chhad parre!' Malik remarked in chaste Punjabi. *Forget it.* He ended the conversation abruptly and left the room.

The reason for the tense atmosphere in the camp and the reference to Dhana became clear to Hamir when he tuned in to Radio Pakistan that evening.

There had been an unfortunate incident at the Indian POW camp at Dhana, Madhya Pradesh. Eight Pakistani POWs had been killed and several injured.

There were contradictory opinions on both sides. Indian authorities attributed it to a failed escape attempt by the POWs while the Pakistani version claimed they were killed in cold blood.

The news had been widely reported in the Pakistani media triggering anger and protests. For the next few days the staff at Lyallpur camp were on edge and the camp atmosphere was extremely tense.

To make matters worse large crowds gathered at the prison gate, baying for the blood of Indian POWs.

The prison authorities had quite a job on their hands. The crowds needed to be controlled. Any violent act against an Indian POW would have disastrous consequences; after all there were more than 90,000 Pakistani POWs in India.

Things had barely settled down in an uneasy calm at Lyallpur when on 13 October another incident occurred in the POW camp at Allahabad, Uttar Pradesh. This time six POWs were killed. As in the previous incident there were again absolutely contrasting narratives from either side.

The local Pakistani print and electronic media once again claimed that it had been a cold-blooded murder by the Indians. Indian media reported that the trigger of the incident was an attempt by Pakistani POWs to grab the personal weapon from an Indian sentry who had then fired in self-defence.

This time there were even larger protests in front of the gate of Lyallpur prison. Crowds gathered throughout the day shouting anti-India slogans. On one occasion the crowd had to be controlled by riot police as they tried to force the prison gates open.

The continuous protests and sloganeering generated a fair degree of tension on the Lyallpur campus. The Indian POWs were asked to remain in their cells for most part of the day and their activities severely restricted.

Things finally settled down when the preparations for Eid commenced towards the end of October.

November 1972

Right from the time when the first Indian POWs arrived at Lyallpur the forty-odd Muslim POWs had been interned away from the Indians of other faiths. Pleas to allow them to reside with the others had fallen on deaf ears.

While the Pakistani authorities would never discuss the issue with the Indians the underlying sentiment was that the Indian Muslim POWs were getting preferential treatment in the camp. It was obvious that the Pakistanis were trying to win over the Indian Muslims, but they were not the lone targets. They had tried the same approach with the Sikhs as well.

Sikh POWs were told that they deserved a separate homeland and Pakistan would help them get it. To play on their sentiments the Sikhs had been taken on visits to Panja Sahib and Nankana Sahib, considered among the holiest of Sikh shrines. In addition the Sikh POWs were the only ones allowed to pray in the gurdwara every Sunday until Hamir had stepped in to extract a similar concession for the Hindus to pray at the mandir.

However, the efforts of the Pakistanis to alter the mindsets of the Sikhs were all in vain. They showed no signs of changing their loyalties. The focus had thereafter shifted to the Indian Muslims.

Since most Indian Muslim POWs belonged to his Charlie Company Hamir and his colleagues were worried on two counts.

Firstly, had the prolonged effort of the Pakistanis affected the soldiers? Secondly, how would the Indian soldiers react when they met the Muslim soldiers, who were believed to be living in better conditions?

Eid-ul-Fitr, the Muslim festival marking the end of a month of fasting, was to be celebrated on 8 November 1972. This would provide the perfect opportunity to find answers to both these questions.

It was decided that the entire camp would join their Muslim colleagues in the Eid prayers. Eid prayers in the prison mosque this year presented a wonderful and moving sight. Close to 600 prisoners joined their fellow Muslims in prayer, irrespective of their religion or faith. The Pakistanis watched in disbelief. After the prayers prisoners hugged each other in the traditional manner and wished each other Eid Mubarak.

There were many moist eyes that day. Doubts of the success of any type of indoctrination were cast away as the Muslim Indian soldiers remained unchanged and unaffected by their seclusion. To the credit of the POWs of the other faiths the preferential treatment given to the Muslim POWs was not held against them and the interaction was enjoyable and without incident.

As a company commander of the Muslim soldiers Hamir was extremely proud of their unflinching loyalty. As the camp senior the maturity the Indian soldiers of other faiths had shown was truly inspiring. Together the Indian POWs had given the Pakistanis a glimpse of the secular nature of India.

~

Towards the third week of November the media was flooded with news about hectic political activity in both India and Pakistan. At Lyallpur there were rumours that a very important person would be visiting soon and he would address all Indian POWs. The camp was spruced up, confirming news of the impending VIP visit.

On the twenty-third of November it was announced that the President of Pakistan Zulfikar Ali Bhutto would be visiting the camp the next day. All POWs were required to be dressed appropriately, and as the seniormost Indian officer, Hamir was to be prepared to have tea with the President. Major Sher Jaman informed Hamir that a message had been received that the Pakistani Chief of Staff General Tikka Khan may also meet him after Mr Bhutto had left.

The next morning a large contingent of journalists and security personnel descended on Lyallpur Jail. At ten o'clock a helicopter could be heard landing near the jail premises. Shortly thereafter sirens announced the arrival of Mr Bhutto.

The jeep carrying Mr Bhutto stopped near the temporary dais that had been set up for his address. The President walked onto the dais and addressed the POWs while the large media contingent took photographs and made notes.

The gist of his talk was that despite the Indian government's intransigence Pakistan had decided to release all Indian POWs unilaterally. The news gladdened the hearts of the POWs but they were still a bit sceptical. Only time would tell whether this would actually happen.

The President left immediately, skipping the tea that had been organized. General Tikka Khan followed suit without interacting with any of the POWs.

Later that evening Sher Jaman met Hamir over tea. The topic turned to the visit of the President and General Tikka Khan. Before the President arrived Sher Jaman had spent some time in General Tikka Khan's company. He had been surprised by the interest Tikka Khan had shown in Hamir's well-being. The general had even insisted that Sher Jaman point Hamir out while he sat in a corner among other POWs, waiting for Bhutto.

Much later in life Hamir realized the connection between General Tikka Khan and his father Maj Gen Kalyan Singh. Tikka Khan and Kalyan Singh had fought together during the Second World War as part of the 2nd Indian Field Regiment. General Tikka Khan had learnt of Hamir's presence in the POW camp and wanted to see the son of his erstwhile colleague, friend and coursemate.

One mystery though remained. Was Tikka Khan then the 'bade officer' that the SM at CMH, Rawalpindi had spoken of? The one who supposedly knew Hamir. Or was it Brigadier Adeeb who he met in Nigeria? Or someone else altogether?

No matter who it was Hamir came to believe that his survival through prison and his repatriation was destiny. He could very easily have been among the more than fifty POWs who never returned to their motherland.[39]

Early on the twenty-fourth of November it was announced that all Indian POWs would be released on 1 December

1972—what Vijay, Hamir's younger son, had in his innocence mentioned in his letter turned out to be true!

~

The next few days were spent on closing of accounts and other documentation.

Each POW was entitled to a monthly allowance depending on their rank. The sepoys and lance naiks were granted Rs 9/- per month while the majors received Rs 60/- per month.

Though less than what Pakistani POWs received in India the allowance primarily covered purchase of essential toiletries from the canteen. Since money was not physically handed over during their stay the balance due after their credit was cleared was required to be calculated. This would now be handed over to them prior to their departure.

On the thirtieth of November all POWs were asked to pack their belongings. It was announced that departure from the camp was scheduled for the evening.

There was an air of excitement in the camp as the POWs gathered their meagre belongings and packed them in whatever bag or packet they could muster. Some, like Hamir, had fabricated suitcases with cardboard and towel material, as part of their creative projects.

In the evening a large number of buses arrived at the camp. The entire lot of over 600 Indians was asked to board the buses which would transport them to Lyallpur Railway Station.

When POWs had arrived at Lyallpur Central Jail they had been blindfolded and handcuffed. In contrast while leaving Lyallpur they boarded the buses without any encumbrances.

Tears of joy flowed easily from the eyes of the POWs as the gates of Lyallpur Jail shut behind them. The fact that they were now on the other side of the prison gates finally dawned upon them.

At Lyallpur Railway Station a special train stood waiting for the POWs. They were escorted into their compartments. By the time the train departed from Lyallpur it was past eight. It had been a long day. The excitement and activity had tired the passengers. Most of them fell asleep in a matter of minutes.

Hamir woke up the next morning at five-thirty. It took him some time to remember that he was on his way home. The train was static. He looked out of his window trying to read the name of the station. The signpost some distance away read Bhagwanpur. Hamir was a bit confused as Bhagwanpura was the name of his own village. He wondered whether he had overslept. *Have I already reached my village?*

The guard standing outside cleared the confusion. He informed him that the train had halted at Bhagwanpur, on the outskirts of Lahore.

The train remained halted at Bhagwanpur, which apparently was its destination. Finally at about nine a convoy of buses arrived and the POWs were soon on the final leg of their journey.

They arrived at the Wagah border crossing point after forty-five minutes. On arrival the POWs were ordered to alight and line up in the order that their names were read out. Moving across the border would be carried out on foot and as per their military ranks. Major Hamir, being the seniormost, would lead the POWs into India.

The sound of a whistle signalled the commencement of the ceremony. Hamir picked up his small white handmade suitcase and commenced walking the final 200 yards into India. He walked proudly leading the column of POWs back to their motherland.

As he stepped over the line marked on the road signifying the international border he turned back to look at Pakistan for a final time.

Many thoughts raced through his mind, including his father's congratulatory letter on being commissioned as an officer in the Indian Army. His father had written, 'I can bear your loss, but not disgrace!'

His father, a veteran of many wars, including the then recent 1962 Sino-Indian War, had experienced loss, witnessed heroism and on a few occasions even seen soldiers bring disgrace. Hamir was certain his father would be anxious to know how his son performed in battle.

One thing was certain. Hamir was alive and his father wouldn't have to bear his loss. But a more serious question was yet to be answered—had he kept the family honour intact?

All the company commanders and senior JCOs who took part in the attack on Daruchhian had either been killed or captured. Therefore the narrative of the disastrous battle had been based on the sole testimony of Lt Col Inderjit. 'As it was, he was almost left out of it, content to command by telephone or radio',[40] 'well behind'[41] from Point 471 on the Indian side, where he was located with his reserves. It was impossible for Inderjit to experience what was actually happening on the ground. He had a lot of explaining to do as his 'over ambitiousness'[42] had resulted in eight officers, seven JCOs and 149 men of other ranks killed, injured or missing in a period of just twelve hours. His narrative was understandably defensive and one-sided. Brigadier Hari Singh had submitted his report of the battle to the higher authorities which presented a contradictory point of view.

It was only the men who had actually fought on the slopes of Daruchhian that fateful morning who would provide the missing part of the puzzle. These men had either died or were captured during the battle. Therefore the Indian Army had been eagerly awaiting the return of the POWs; their debriefing would unravel the details of the Battle of Daruchhian. The debriefing reports, Hamir hoped, would settle once and for all whether he had brought disgrace to his father.

He had fought hard and bravely at Daruchhian, this he was certain of. But it was the testimony of the other returning POWs that would reveal the truth.

Engrossed as he was in these thoughts the poignancy of returning to his motherland was lost on Hamir.

Part Four

HOMECOMING

1 December 1972, 11:00 Hours. Wagah,[43] Punjab

Bharat Mata ki Jai! Bharat Mata ki Jai! Vande Matram![44]

The shouting of slogans and beating of drums by a large crowd instantaneously brought Hamir back into the moment. He was the first one to emerge onto the Indian side through the gates of the India–Pakistan border at Wagah.

Hamir being welcomed by Giani Zail Singh.
Photo courtesy of Ministry of Defence, History Division.

Giani Zail Singh, the then chief minister of the state of Punjab in India, garlanded him in traditional welcome. The Chief Minister pulled him close and hugged him tightly to the delight of the waiting press. Whether it was the emotion of the moment or the need to allow the press photographers time, Giani Zail Singh's embrace seemed longer than required, making Hamir self-conscious besides causing physical discomfort.

Senior army officers were the next to welcome him. Far in the distance Hamir could see his father waiting patiently, scanning the crowd, looking for his son.

Hamir hadn't expected his father at Wagah. It was a pleasant surprise, and on finding him there he couldn't wait to meet him. But before he could have a reunion with his father he had to go through the formalities of shaking hands with the long line of dignitaries who formed part of the official welcome. His injured right hand had now begun to hurt because of the large number of enthusiastic handshakes he had endured. Finally he had reached the end of the line and he shook hands with the last official.

Relieved, Hamir hurried towards his father only to be surprised by the sudden appearance of Lt Col Inderjit, who inquired about his well-being. After a brief and formal exchange Hamir was free to meet his father and headed in his direction. The moment he got closer the old man recognized his son. He smiled with joy and thrust his hand forward attempting an awkward formal handshake. Hamir would have none of it—he hugged his father, perhaps for the first time in his adult life. His father was equally emotional, in front of his son, perhaps for the first time in his life.

Letting go of his son from an awkward embrace he tentatively examined Hamir's right hand. 'No amputation?' he remarked, relieved.

'No amputation,' Hamir replied, confirming his father's observation.

'Thank goodness. Does it hurt?'

'No, not really. I don't have total control yet; I can't close my fist entirely. They said it will be fine with physiotherapy.'

'I am sure it will be fine.'

They conversed for a while. Maj Gen Kalyan Singh had spent sleepless nights thinking of his son. Now that Hamir was back he was relieved and happy. If he had any anxiety about the future of his son it didn't show on his face.

Lunch had been organized at Wagah itself. While the POWs ate the delicious food on offer they were swamped by journalists and happy family members. The Punjab state government had gone out of its way to make the prisoners feel special and they revelled in the attention.

After lunch the returnees were asked to board buses which would take them to Amritsar city where a grand reception had been planned in the evening. The 20-kilometre drive was a part of the celebratory welcome. The buses passed through numerous welcome arches. The roadsides were decorated with flags and festoons. Men, women and children cheered as the buses made their way to the reception site.

The civic reception was well attended and thousands cheered as each officer was felicitated on the stage. They were garlanded and presented with gifts and sweets. Long-winded speeches by the Chief Minister and others followed in what was a rather long ceremony.

The reception culminated with dinner during which dignitaries interacted with the returnees. After dinner the air force officers split ways from their army colleagues. A special plane had been requisitioned to take them to Palam Airport in Delhi. The rest of the returnees were taken to Amritsar Railway station where a Military Special Train awaited to take them to Delhi Cantonment.

The special train left Amritsar Railway Station on the night of 1 December 1972 carrying in it over 600 former POWs, each one more excited than the other, in anticipation of what would be a reunion with their family after almost a year.

2 December 1972. Delhi Cantonment Railway Station

The otherwise quiet and desolate Delhi Cantt Railway Station bustled with activity in preparation of the grand arrival of the returnees from Pakistan. Since early in the morning a large number of railway staff had been busy cleaning the station.

Tables lined the platform in military order, crisp white tablecloth draped on them. White enamel military mugs lay upside down along both sides of the numerous tables laid out on Platform Number 1. The spartan decorations with flower vases which were essentially empty Fanta[45] bottles, rather ingeniously improvised in true army style, added colour to the festivities.

Balloons, festoons and flags provided the station a festive look. CMP personnel and policemen regulated entry as a large crowd was anticipated. TV cameras were placed at strategic locations.

By about nine the station was crowded with people anxiously waiting for the arrival of the Military Special. The Rajputana Rifles band played military tunes entertaining the waiting crowd.

The aroma of tea and freshly fried jalebis filled the air. The laying out of tea and refreshments suggested that the train was about to arrive. Shortly thereafter an announcement was made that the Military Special had arrived. The crowds cheered as the whistling steam engine slowly came to a halt at the platform.

The POWs seated in the train waved enthusiastically to the crowd through the train windows as they eagerly looked for their near and dear ones.

Soon the welcome ceremony was underway. The band began marching, leading the Chief of Army Staff General S.H.F.J. Manekshaw, who waved to his soldiers as he moved in front of each bogey.

The platform was filled with cheers and laughter. Politicians with their supporters marched around the platform shouting 'Bharat Mata ki jai!' Photographers and journalists jostled with each other taking photos and seeking interviews.

Laxmi stood on one corner of the platform silently observing the proceedings, a bit overwhelmed by the large crowd. Vijay tugged at her saree, excitedly pointing to the steam engine which had halted just next to where they stood.

In her elegant silk saree Laxmi stood out among a sea of uniforms. She strained her eyes scanning the platform, her face reflecting her anxiety. It had been some time since the train had arrived; she hadn't been able to spot her husband yet.

The movement control officer (MCO) walked up to her; he could see the worry on her face.

'The officers' compartment is in the middle of the train ma'am, you need to move ahead if you are looking for your husband,' he said.

Laxmi caught hold of her children's hands and hurried forward. They must have walked about twenty yards when Vikram shouted—'Mama, look there, its papa!'

Before she realized Vikram let go of Laxmi's hand and ran towards a tall, thin man whose right hand was bandaged. Vijay

Hamir with his wife Laxmi and two sons, Vikram and Vijay, at the Delhi Cantt Railway Station. Photo courtesy of Ministry of Defence, History Division.

followed suit. Laxmi followed her children. *No way, he cannot be my husband*, she thought. He is way too thin. Whatever doubts she had were cast aside the moment the man hugged her children. It was Hamir indeed.

She rushed to join them. Their small family was finally together again. Though emotional, both Hamir and Laxmi greeted each other formally, conscious of the onlookers.

A posse of journalists rushed towards them; they had been looking to interview the seniormost officer. The journalist from All India Radio thrust a microphone towards Laxmi, eager to record her feelings.

Meanwhile the newspaper reporters, eager to obtain a photo of the family reunion for the morning headlines, insisted Hamir lift Vijay up. The fact that Hamir had a bandaged hand didn't bother them at all. If anything, it would provide greater significance to the photo. Realizing that the only way to get rid of them was to oblige them Hamir picked Vijay up for a very short moment. The journalists, satisfied, finally left the family alone.

But privacy was hard to come by. Hamir's colleagues from the POW camp were eager to meet the child who had predicted their repatriation. Hamir directed them towards Vijay, who had now become the centre of attraction. Vijay giggled excitedly as he was flung in the air and passed around the group of officers. Vikram watched in amusement.

Laxmi and Hamir continued to receive well-wishers. While they recognized some of them most were unknown, simply happy to welcome their soldiers back.

Through the crowd Hamir could see the prominent white hackle of the Grenadiers. A young soldier made his way towards them. Accompanying the soldier was an elderly gentleman who was dressed in dhoti and kurta. He looked dishevelled in contrast to the smartly turned out jawan accompanying him.

'Ram Ram, sahab! I am Grenadier Shamshad Ali,[46] 14 Grenadiers.'

'Ram Ram!' Hamir replied. He couldn't quite place the young soldier. 'How are you?'

'Absolutely fine, sir,' the jawan replied. 'This is Lieutenant Dalal's father. He was waiting eagerly to meet you.'

Hamir instantly understood the reason for the elderly man's obvious sadness. As he looked towards him the old man folded his hands in greeting.

'Ram Ram, sahab! I am Omi's father.' Om Prakash Dalal was perhaps called Omi at home.

'Ram Ram, sir,' he replied a bit gingerly, he wasn't prepared for this meeting.

'You have come back. Can you tell me when my son will return?' his hands remained folded, almost as if he was pleading.

Hamir looked towards Shamshad. How was it possible that the old man didn't know about his son's death till now? Shamshad just shrugged his shoulders.

Hamir wrapped his hands around the old man's folded hands.

'He was a very brave boy, sir. He fought with me right till the very end. I only wish I could have got him back with me!'

'Don't worry, sahab, I am certain he will be back.' Tears were streaming down the old man's face.

'I know how it feels, sir, but I am afraid Omi won't be coming back!'

'No! Please don't say that. He's still breathing somewhere. Our village priest swears that Omi is still alive.'

Hamir didn't know what to say.

'Sahab, when you left him did you check his breathing or his pulse. Babaji is one hundred per cent sure he's still alive. He told me so.'

The old man wasn't ready to believe his son was dead.

'Did you see him dead yourself? Are you absolutely sure?' he continued.

The question took Hamir back to the battle on the slopes of Daruchhian. He could see Dalal lying wounded on West Spur after having been instrumental in defeating the enemy's first attack; their unsuccessful attempts to revive him and the horrible feeling of helplessness as Dalal's life slowly ebbed away.

'Yes, sir. Sadly, he died before my eyes. You are the proud father of a very brave martyr, sir.'

He felt helpless and miserable. *How do I convince his father that his son is dead? I wish we could have recovered his dead body*, he thought.

'No, no! It's not possible. He can't die! He promised me he would return. I know he's alive somewhere. I will prove all you people wrong. I will get him back from wherever he is...' he said in between sobs as he walked away leaving Hamir speechless.

Laxmi, who had been observing closely all along, had tears in her eyes. The exchange between Hamir and the old man had exposed her to the plight of the kith and kin of the many soldiers who would never get the opportunity to meet their family again. God had been kind to her. Hamir was back. She gripped Hamir's hand tightly as the old man disappeared into the crowd.

Lieutenant Dalal's father wouldn't get over the loss of his son for a very long time. He was a regular visitor to Hamir's residence for more than a year. On each visit he would bring with him what he considered authentic information, provided by some baba or the other that his son was alive. Each visit brought back unpleasant memories leaving Hamir and Laxmi saddened by the grief of the unfortunate father.

'Mama, I want jalebi! I want jalebi!' Vikram was hopping up and down.

'Haan, me too. Jalebi, jalebi, jalebi, please...!' Vijay had an annoying habit of mimicking his brother; he was hopping up and down too.

'OK, OK. Chalo, let's go.' Laxmi herded the boys towards the nearest table where the eats had been laid out.

The sumptuous spread disappeared in quick time as hungry crowds devoured the delicious eats. The moment tea was served an announcement was made asking for the returnees to board the waiting vehicles which would take them to the transit camp.

The officers were taken to the Territorial Army Officers'

Mess on Parade Road, Delhi Cantonment. The debriefing, which was to commence the next day, had the stringent requirement for the returnees to be kept isolated.

Laxmi had decided to move in with some family friends in Delhi. The children would return to Alwar so that they wouldn't miss school.

3 December 1972, 08:00 Hours.
Debriefing Room, Delhi Cantonment

Debriefing of repatriated prisoners is a very important process as it serves a number of purposes. Firstly, it helps ascertain the mental health and general well-being of the returning soldier. The debriefing officer is required to comment on the degree of indoctrination, if any, he finds in the repatriated prisoner. From the point of view of battle reports the debriefing also fills in gaps of information. The findings of a debriefing could help identify a cowardly act or form the basis of a citation for a heretofore unrecognized act of bravery.

Since the repatriated soldiers had spent considerable time in the POW camp the debriefing would also ascertain their actions and behaviour during their internment. The team put together for this sensitive task was selected diligently, ensuring the inclusion of officers of adequate seniority and maturity.

The debriefing of the repatriated POWs of the 1962 Sino-Indian War had gone on for almost six months during which they were not allowed to interact with their family members. This had generated a lot of unhappiness, bad blood and adverse publicity. While welcoming the returnees at Delhi Cantt railway station General Manekshaw had promised that this time the debriefing would be completed in less than three weeks.

Given the enormity of the task the debriefing team had been organized in an efficient manner. Led by a colonel the team consisted of a few majors belonging to various branches of the army. Some JCOs had been included in the team to debrief the other ranks.

Each person would be debriefed individually. While being debriefed returnees were expected to refrain from interacting with fellow returnees so that the account constructed on the basis of respective testimonies could be as objective as possible.

Each evening reports of the debriefing would be collated and handed over to the colonel who would go over the dossier of each expatriated soldier, appending his remarks.

Given that there were more than 600 returnees the process was expected to take a reasonable amount of time. Therefore the debriefing would commence early every day and go on till late at night.

Being the seniormost Hamir was the first officer to be debriefed. The debriefing was exhausting. Recalling the events brought back painful memories and the questions asked were often irritating and intrusive.

The officer responsible for debriefing Hamir was professional, diligent and well prepared. It was apparent that he had made notes while studying the available battle reports prior to the debriefing as he referred to them often during the process.

Hamir's testimony was vital in delivering closure to an attack that had failed, hence the debriefing officer's deliberation was understandable. His version of events would be compared with the debriefing report of soldiers who had been captured while fighting alongside Hamir.

His debriefing lasted almost ten hours after which an exhausted Hamir was allowed to return to his room. He would now be summoned, if required, during the debriefing of some other soldier or on conclusion of the entire process. He was now permitted to meet Laxmi.

When they met after his debriefing it was the first time that they were together alone. In the privacy of their room Hamir hugged Laxmi tightly.

'Sapana,' he said, 'you know, I had said goodbye to you during the battle on the morning of the fourteenth of December. I was certain I would die. I can't believe I am back with you!'

'And I thought I had lost you when Vikram had the most

terrible nightmare about you. Thank God, you are back!'

Laxmi studied Hamir's wounds closely. The top of his right hand had scars of the bullets which had pierced through the outer part of his biceps. His forearm had multiple scars due to bullet injuries as well as stitches from the many operations that he had undergone. His hand looked unnaturally thin.

While awake, Hamir would constantly exercise his wrist by moving it either in an up-down or rotational movement. This therapeutic exercise had almost become involuntary and he would do it subconsciously.

During the debriefings, meeting Laxmi, whenever permitted, provided Hamir the much required relief from negative thoughts or bad memories that would surface sometimes. Their meetings were mostly one-sided conversations with Laxmi filling him in with details of the past year. Conversations would be interspersed with tears when Laxmi recalled some unpleasant memory, or laughter, when funny anecdotes concerning the children were recounted.

Laxmi knew very little of what Hamir had been through in the previous year. Whenever the subject came up Hamir would change the topic. The little that she knew were the incidental bits and pieces she had picked up during Hamir's conversations with senior officers who would visit him from time to time. After every such conversation she would notice a change in Hamir's behaviour. He would turn unusually quiet and withdrawn. In due course she learned to recognize his darker moods, when it was best to leave him alone. On such occasions he would remain edgy and forlorn for the rest of the day.

It had been almost a week and Laxmi hadn't made headway into Hamir's innermost thoughts. She felt that the best way to rid Hamir of his stress was to talk about it.

It had been an enjoyable Sunday and they had spent the whole day together. He was in a good mood. It was almost time for him to return. Laxmi decided to make her move. She handed him his cup of tea, placed some biscuits beside him and sat opposite, holding her cup of tea.

'I hope the sugar is fine?'

'Perfect, Sapana, like you!' he replied, smiling.

'I have a suggestion to make.'

'Oh really? And what is that?' Hamir said, intrigued, not knowing where the conversation was headed.

'You know they say whenever you have some bad memories, it's best to let them out. At least that's what Kanwarsa says!' Laxmi remarked.

Hamir went quiet and the change in his expression made Laxmi nervous. She seemed to have touched a raw nerve. But now there was no way out, she had to finish what she had started.

'Why don't you share your bad memories with me?' she pleaded tentatively.

'OK, Sapana, I will try,' he said, hoping it might help unburden himself.

'Please, please do!' Laxmi said, relieved.

'The incident occurred a few hours before I was captured. We were caught in the open under some extremely heavy artillery shelling. We looked for safety in the scarce natural cover that was available. Some of the men were panic-stricken.'

Laxmi was terrified but still curious. Hamir continued, 'Amidst the shelling, one of my youngest soldiers, hardly eighteen or nineteen years old, comes running to me. He's shivering with fright and yells out—Sahab, bahut darr lag raha hai! Mujhe bacha lo. Meri maa akeli hai, unka aur koi nahin hai. Woh akeli nahin reh payegi!

'Get down, take cover, I ordered! It's dangerous to remain in the open! But frozen out of fear he remained standing. He kept repeating what he had said as if I could work a spell. And then there's this massive blast just next to where he was standing. Worried, I look towards him.'

Hamir closed his eyes for a while trying to control his emotions. It wasn't working. Laxmi waited patiently allowing Hamir the time he needed to continue.

'I look towards him and I see his feet firmly anchored on the ground but when I look up there's nothing left of his upper body...'

He stopped speaking and shut his eyes, reliving the pain of the memory. Laxmi was overcome with emotion as well. She had caught a glimpse of what her husband had experienced and felt miserable dragging him back into the hell that he had been through. She reached out to him and tenderly cradled his head, quietly whispering an apology to him. Simply letting bad memories out might not be the best way to get rid of them, she thought.

He remained seated, his eyes still shut. It was quite a while before he regained his composure. But hard as he tried he couldn't get rid of some difficult questions. *Should I have done something differently? Could I have saved any of them? Why am I even alive?*

He knew he had done the best he could. And also that maybe Laxmi was right. Talking about it could perhaps help him. But not now. The wounds were too raw and the debriefing had made it worse! He needed time to heal.

Laxmi understood. She decided that she herself would never raise the subject again. It was a promise she has kept. She counted her blessings with immense gratitude—her husband was alive and that's all that mattered.

14 December 1972, 09:00 Hours.
Debriefing Room, Delhi Cantonment

It had been more than two weeks since the commencement of the debriefings. The previous evening the officers had been told that the concluding interviews with the debriefing team were scheduled for the next day. After that they would all be granted leave.

Hamir's interview was scheduled at 09:00 hours and he entered the colonel's office accordingly.

'Good morning, sir.'

'Good morning, Major, please take a seat.'

Hamir settled into his chair waiting anxiously for what the colonel had to say. The colonel drew out Hamir's dossier from the drawer, put on his reading glasses and flipped through its pages.

'Major, you are aware, over the last two weeks my team and I have debriefed over 600 men.'

'Yes, sir,' Hamir replied.

'We interviewed men from your unit, 14 Grenadiers, as well as others who were POWs with you at Lyallpur.'

'Yes, sir.'

'And of course the six army officers,' the colonel added.

'Yes, sir, that's correct.'

'We have a fairly good idea what happened to your company on Daruchhian and what transpired at Lyallpur POW Camp.'

'I suppose so, sir,' said Hamir, unaware of the turn of the conversation.

'I need to compliment you on two counts,' the colonel continued.

'Sir?'

'Firstly, every prisoner with you at Lyallpur has acknowledged the positive impact of your leadership. They say that ever since you arrived at the camp, you made a material difference to their physical and mental well-being. My congratulations. I have endorsed that in my remarks here,' the colonel stated.

'Thank you, sir, but I was just doing my duty as the senior officer among them,' Hamir said, with becoming modesty.

'I am not finished yet. I salute your bravery, Major,' he said, as he continued speaking. 'Your comrades have provided us with the missing pieces of the Daruchhian battle. You showed amazing bravery throughout the battle. Absolute madness, charging up the mountain top in broad daylight! And with a badly injured hand and no weapon! What were you thinking? It's a miracle you are alive!' He was effusive in his praise.

'How could I send my men on an attack without leading them? I don't know how and why I am alive, but to be honest, I sometimes feel guilty that I am alive!' Hamir replied, humbled by the colonel's compliments.

'Really proud of you, Major. I am sure everyone who reads my report will be proud too. I am recommending you for the highest of the gallantry awards. You deserve no less. I only hope the authorities that matter recognize your courage, despite the debacle at Daruchhian,' the colonel said with sincerity.

'Thank you, sir. If I lived up to my men's expectations, I have got my award. That's the important thing,' Hamir replied. 'But I have a request.'

'Sure, Major, go ahead. What can I do for you?'

'My comrades, sir. I am not sure whether their bravery has been established in your findings, but I can vouch for their heroic actions. They had an important role to play in the little success we achieved at Daruchhian.'

'Of course, please give me their names.'

> Gdr RUKUMUDIN of C Coy 14 GRENADIERS went with the coy to attack on SW SPUR of DARUCHIAN POST of the enemy on night 13/14 Dec 71. He was LMG No-1 in one of the leading secs of the coy. Inspite of heavy enemy SA and Arty fire on the attacking tps he kept on moving ahead and reached the SW SPUR ahead of the coy. He kept on firing with his LMG from hip position till he reached top then he made the enemy to fled and the coy occupied SW SPUR. Later when the enemy heavily shelled the coy posn and counter attacked the coy posn, Gdr RUKUMUDIN was seriously injured on the leg by shell splinters. But he kept on manning his LMG post and kept on firing at his long killing several enemy. The enemy counter attacked the posn three times but he remained clung to his LMG till he became unconscious due to heavy bleeding. He showed great valour and devotion to duty.
>
> Gdr AST ALI — C.Cy 14 GRENADIERS.
> Capt OP DALAL

Citation written in Hamir's hand for a colleague who fought beside him.

The colonel duly noted the names in his diary, and requested Hamir to write their citations before he left. The interview over, he shook Hamir's hand and bid him farewell, wishing him the best for the future.

Hamir left the colonel's office relieved. His actions during the battle stood vindicated. His return would not be in disgrace.

~

The next day Hamir reported to Base Hospital for a medical review. After examining his hand the doctors concluded that the Pakistanis had done a reasonably good job and there was nothing more to be done. He was classified as a permanent medical category and granted medical leave.

Hamir and Laxmi headed to Hamir's paternal village—Bhagwanpura. He looked forward to meeting his mother and his elder brother Himmat and younger brother Pushpendra. Their arrival at Bhagwanpura was greeted with joyous celebrations. Visitors from neighbouring villages gathered in large numbers to welcome the brave son of the already legendary General Kalyan Singh.

After paying obeisance at the Kuldevi's mandir Hamir was pampered silly by his mother who had lovingly prepared all his favourite dishes, including lal maas, his very favourite.

Nawa, the closest town to Bhagwanpura held a civic reception in Hamir's honour. He was paraded through the streets in an open jeep as part of a celebratory convoy of vehicles. People lined up on the streets to garland Hamir and shower him with flower petals. He was now a local hero.

Inherently shy, he was a bit overawed by the welcome. For a person happy in deflecting attention, getting used to his new-found status took some time.

The idyllic rural setting at Bhagwanpura proved to be the perfect place to recoup. Hamir spent happy, carefree days roaming the fields, meeting up with old friends and acquaintances. By the time he reported back to Army Base Hospital, Delhi after a month, he was mentally and physically much better. His medical formalities were completed in a couple of days and he was free to rejoin duty.

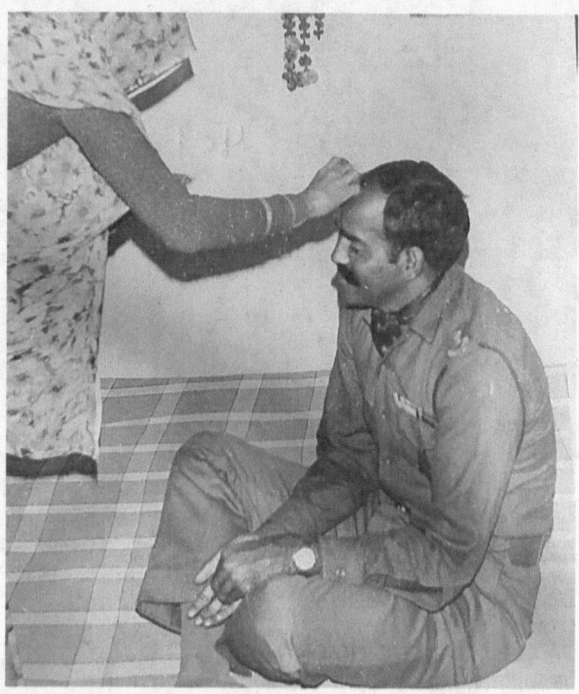

Hamir being welcomed home in the traditional manner.

Each POW was allowed to choose where he would like to be posted. Hamir chose Jaipur. Accordingly he was posted to 61 (Independent) Sub Area Jaipur.

One of the first things Hamir did on arrival at Jaipur was to visit the brand new road connecting the cantonment to the city. The road had been named Kalyan Marg to honour his father Maj Gen Kalyan Singh on his retirement. His heart swelled with pride reading the plaque bearing his father's name.

After spending a few days settling down Hamir joined his new workplace. Work was easy paced and peaceful. It was January, and winter in Rajasthan is the best season. Back with his family Hamir enjoyed spending quality time with Laxmi and the children. He would take them to tourist attractions in and around Jaipur followed by outdoor picnics. These excursions on his brand new Lambretta scooter were fun filled and enjoyable. Days passed by uneventfully.

Photos of the hero's welcome Hamir received at Nawa.

Homecoming

It was the ceremonial season in Delhi. Army Day had been celebrated on 15 January and it was 26 January 1973, India's Republic Day.

Hamir sat out in the verandah enjoying a cup of tea while reading the newspapers. An inconspicuous news item on the last page of the newspaper caught his eye. 'Gallantry Awards Announced', it said. The article contained a list of officers who had been awarded gallantry awards on the eve of Republic Day 1973. Among the names was Major Hamir Singh, 14 Grenadiers and Captain J.C. Gosain, 196 Mountain Regiment. Both had been awarded the Vir Chakra.

The awards connected to the 1971 Indo-Pakistan War had already been announced the previous year. The gallantry awards awarded to Hamir and Gosain were based on the findings and recommendations of the team that had conducted the debriefing of the repatriated POWs.

Hamir had all but forgotten his conversation during his final interview with the colonel who had conducted his debriefing at Delhi. The news of being awarded certainly came as a wonderful surprise. He shared the news with Laxmi, whose joy knew no bounds. They decided to keep it to themselves until official intimation was received.

It didn't take too long, however, for the official communication to arrive. Hamir and Laxmi were soon besieged by a flood of congratulatory calls and messages. There were celebrations again as friends and relatives descended to their house at Pratap Lines, Jaipur.

April 1973. Rashtrapati Bhawan, New Delhi

Rashtrapati Bhawan, one of the most beautiful monuments of Lutyens' Delhi, was hosting the Defence Investiture Ceremony.

It was a cool April evening and a large crowd of invitees waited patiently for the security staff to let them in. Hamir and Laxmi, being special guests, were ushered directly to the Durbar Hall, where the ceremony would be conducted.

Laxmi looked resplendent in her blue floral chiffon saree.

Her beautiful face radiant with pride and happiness as she sat waiting for the ceremony to begin. Dressed in his crisp summer ceremonial uniform Hamir looked dashingly smart.

The Durbar Hall, located under the massive central dome of the President's house, was a breathtaking venue. Traditionally host to formal events the massive pillars and giant banners provided an impressive backdrop.

Within minutes the 500-odd seats available were occupied by the who's who of the nation. Prime Minister Indira Gandhi and her cabinet ministers had already arrived and were seated next to the chiefs of the army, navy and air force. Field Marshal Manekshaw was busy interacting with people in his flamboyant style when the trumpets signalling the President's arrival were sounded.

The gathering hushed to silence as President V.V. Giri entered the Durbar Hall, escorted by his smartly turned out ADCs. He was led right up to the stage on which his chair had been placed. The imposing statue of Lord Buddha stood behind him as he took his seat facing the large gathering.

The ceremony commenced with citations being read in English and Hindi after which each awardee marched up smartly to receive their medals from the President.

In a few minutes it was Hamir's turn. His citation was read out and as Hamir marched to receive his award he was greeted by thunderous applause. Laxmi clapped as loudly as she could.

The ceremony was over in about an hour, after which the awardees were free to interact with the audience. Prime Minister Gandhi moved from awardee to awardee, congratulating them. She approached Hamir and Laxmi. The young wife of an awardee had probably caught her attention.

'Well done, Major, we are really proud of you,' she remarked. 'And is this young lady the woman behind your success?'

'Yes, ma'am!' was all that Hamir could mumble. Field Marshal Manekshaw, accompanying Mrs Gandhi, stood smiling at Laxmi.

It was a proud moment for the young couple. They

President V.V. Giri conferring the
Vir Chakra on Hamir.

Hamir and Laxmi with Indira Gandhi at Rashtrapati Bhawan.
Laxmi proudly holding the award in her hands.

graciously accepted the felicitations of the many VVIPs who greeted them.

In the midst of this Hamir suddenly heard a lady call out his name.

'Excuse me, are you Major Hamir Singh?'

'Yes, ma'am, that's correct.'

Hamir realized that she was Mrs Gosain. He had seen her receive the Vir Chakra on behalf of her husband.

'I am Mrs Gosain, wife of Captain J.C. Gosain.'

'Yes, ma'am, I know, I saw you receive his award. Gosain was among the bravest men I know. We fought together till the very end.'

'I know, Major.' He could see that she was close to tears.

'I want to know how he died. No one has given me a clear answer. You were there with him, weren't you?' she asked.

'Yes, I was there. Like I said, he died a hero,' Hamir replied, wishing she would leave the topic alone. But gave in when she insisted.

Having heard from her husband's colleague about the last moments of his life, Mrs Gosain took her leave with one final look at Hamir. An officer of 196 Mountain Regiment escorted her protectively as she made her way through the crowd. Hamir watched silently till he could see her no more.

He looked sad and Laxmi realized that his interaction with Gosain's widow had been equally unpleasant for him. She slid her palm into Hamir's hand and tugged gently.

'Chalo, we need to leave,' she said, as she led her husband out.

Hamir followed Laxmi mechanically, his face expressionless as they moved out. They were soon back in their car and on their journey to Dholpur.

The journey would take over six hours, time enough for Hamir to reflect on the events of the day. He remained quiet and withdrawn. It had been an emotionally draining day.

Laxmi was very tired and it wasn't long before she fell asleep. Hamir, of course, was lost in his thoughts, flitting alternatively between Daruchhian and Durbar Hall.

Why am I even alive? Why wasn't I killed as I climbed the slopes of Daruchhian in broad daylight? Why didn't my captors shoot me dead?

He was among the very few survivors of the battle at Daruchhian. As company commander he had seen so many of his beloved comrades die next to him. He had witnessed the heroism of his men, even when things didn't go their way. He was the only person who had seen what really happened on the slopes of Daruchhian that fateful night.

How would the fathers, mothers, wives, children or battalions of soldiers such as Dalal, Gosain, Taj Mohammad or Rukmuddin ever learn about the sacrifices that their loved ones had made in doing their duty?

A sudden thought struck him. *Maybe that was it! The purpose of my survival. The larger purpose in God's scheme of things.*

Someday, when he's up to it, he would tell their story. He owed it to his men.

He glanced out of his window. In the far distance beyond the Yamuna the Taj Mahal glistened, looking magnificent in the rays of setting sun.

Maybe, the story, when it's finally told, will be my Taj Mahal to the memory of the brave soldiers of Charlie Company, 14 Grenadiers who remained Sarvada Shaktishali till they were martyred.

It's taken fifty years...

Epilogue

25 January 2005. Jaipur

'Has it arrived?' my mother inquires. 'You have already taken ten rounds since morning.'

'No, not yet. I suppose it will be here by evening,' my father replies, somewhat miffed.

The conversation refers to the invite my father gets for the annual Governor's 'At Home', on the occasion of Republic Day. During the event the Governor interacts with eminent people over a high tea. Attended by a large number of prominent personalities, many look forward to the function for purposes of networking. Some take pride in the fact that they are among the glitterati of Jaipur. To others, like my father, it is recognition of their service to their beloved country in some field or the other.

The 'At Home' and preparation preceding it is an annual ritual for my father. He diligently takes out his Nehru coat, ensures it is spotlessly clean and wrinkle free. He then takes out his miniature medals and pins them up on the suit. Next is his mandatory haircut and grooming of his proud moustache. Last but not the least is his Rajput saafa which is washed and then starched until it feels absolutely crisp on his fingers, making it easy for him to tie it himself.

I've got to grant it to my old man. The painstaking preparations are not in vain; when he finally dresses up, wearing all the paraphernalia, he is indeed a handsome sight—resplendent in his immaculate turnout. But what actually gives him the edge is the pride with which he dons his 'post-retirement uniform' as he likes to call it.

Epilogue

Our house at Amba Bari, Jaipur is a double-storied one. My parents live upstairs, which means accessing the post box is a walk down the staircase and thereafter a walk of approximately fifteen metres to the gate, next to which is the post box.

My mother is obviously irritated by my father's enthusiasm for the invite. After his umpteenth visit to the post box she suggests:

'Listen, it's already 25th. If it had to come it should have been here by now. Why don't you speak to someone?'

The suggestion sparks an idea. He glances through the Telephone Directory, finds the number to the Governor's secretariat and dials the number. Many long rings later the call is picked up.

'Yes.' A lady operator's voice is heard at the other end.

'Is that the Governor's Office?' my father questions.

'Yes, that's right. How can I help you?' the lady answers.

'Good morning. I am a retired army officer, Brigadier Hamir Singh.'

'Good morning, sir. What can I do for you?'

'You see I haven't got my invite to the "At Home" yet. I was wondering whether you have misplaced my address or something. I normally get it by this time of the year.'

'Wait, sir, let me check. Brigadier Hamir Singh...hmm, let's see... I am afraid, sir, your name isn't on the list of invitees. You know, sir, this year we have gone through the list with a tooth comb. We need to downsize the event. We really have to adjust with such a growing number of VVIPs, senior bureaucrats, etc...'

'I see,' my father replies without any noticeable disappointment in his voice.

The lady adds in retrospect—'Unless of course you have done something extraordinary for the country—have you?'

The lady is sounding almost impertinent.

'No, not really. Nothing extraordinary. Just fought for the country when called to—but that's our job, I guess. Thank you. You have been most helpful.'

I don't think she really registered my father's reply. Or if she did, she didn't really care. She had work to do and could do without useless grumbling.

'You are welcome, sir, we will try to adjust you during our Iftar or Diwali parties...'

'No, thank you, that won't be necessary. Good evening.'

My father hangs up. Mama looks at my father. He can't hide the disappointment on his face, at least not from the discerning eye of my mother.

'What happened?'

'Nothing really. They misplaced the address actually...' He lies, knowing for sure that his lie wouldn't stand muster with my mom.

Mama doesn't want to embarrass the old war horse any more.

'It's OK, I guess. As it is, it's such a distance away, reaching there would have been a hassle. We'll just watch the Republic Day Parade on TV.'

Undoubtedly, my father was disappointed.

The 'At Home' with its mouth-watering delicacies and opportunity for hobnobbing with celebrities never caught his fancy. Neither did he look forward to the opportunities for networking. In so many years of attending the function he had never once narrated his war experiences to anyone. He never felt the need to explain his presence among the many luminaries. He was content in his own company, moving around with his shiny medals pinned proudly to his chest.

Now this is the part most people, other than those in the defence forces, may find hard to understand. Yes, the person wearing the medals is proud of his achievements, but that's not the only reason behind the obvious pride with which he wears them. The medals are an acknowledgment of the unquestioned loyalty and bravery of his comrades, without which the achievement would not be possible. The entire platoon, company or unit has contributed in some measure in the individual being decorated. With my father it is no different. He wears his Vir Chakra with pride, dedicated to the gallantry of the men of Charlie Company, 14 Grenadiers, who willingly gave their lives in doing what their company commander asked them to do.

There are thousands of old soldiers in our country, peacefully retired, happy to remain in the background while they catch up with the simplest of pleasures they missed during their service. They don't seek recognition; in fact many of them would be embarrassed if you would want to acknowledge them in any way. But they do imbibe pleasure when an occasional nicety is shown to them. Little gestures to give them the assurance that the nation hasn't forgotten them.

My father got his little dose of pleasure being invited for the 'At Home'.

He walks down to his neighbour, his younger brother, Colonel Pushpendra Singh's house.

Pushi, as he is lovingly called, is the kid brother of my dad. With an age difference of over ten years my father really dotes on him. One of the reasons perhaps why Pushi got married to my mother's younger sister Manu. All in the family, as they say.

Colonel Pushpendra was commissioned in 45 Cavalry and later commanded 8 Cavalry, after which he sought premature retirement. A commando dagger, a thorough gentleman with a hands-on approach to life, Pushpendra is fondly remembered by the men of both his regiments, even today, many years after having hung up his uniform.

'Pushi, I am not going for the "At Home" this year,' declares my father as he eases himself into a seat in the veranda.

'Kyun, dada, what happened?' Pushpendra replies, a bit surprised.

'Just like that. Not in the mood really!' My father is in no mood to elaborate.

'So...'

'Pushi, why don't we go to the war memorial tomorrow morning instead?'

'No problem, what time?'

'10:00 hours maybe,' my father replies.

'Right. What about bhabhi and Manu?'

'They can come too. It will be a good outing for them as well.'

'Fine. I will tell her, dada,' Pushi remarks.

'OK. See you then. I better get my stuff ready.' He gets up and heads back home.

The twenty-sixth of January. It's about a quarter to ten in the morning. Pushpendra takes out his car from the garage and parks it momentarily on the road, ready, waiting for his dada and bhabhi. The co-driver's seat is vacant for his brother. Manu is seated behind the driver's seat, waiting for her sister to join her.

My father and mother are hurrying down towards the car. Mama is under pressure, running a bit late, doing her little things. The obvious impatience of my father bugging her, perhaps making her nervous. She is having trouble locking the door.

Meanwhile loud honking is heard as a shiny new car driven by a youngster looks for the right of way, which is somewhat blocked by Colonel Pushpendra's car. Pushpendra looks over his shoulder and indicates to the driver to hang on a second. But it only results in even more frenzied honking.

My father and mother move at the best possible speed towards the car. The young driver is by now livid, seated next to his young wife.

He yells at Colonel Pushpendra. 'Hurry up, uncle, are you deaf or something?'

My uncle is normally a patient man. He seems annoyed by the fact that the young man doesn't have the decency to wait for an elderly couple.

He replies, 'Really in a hurry, eh? Can't you see the elderly people taking their seats in the car? Are you blind or just an idiot?'

The driver would have none of it. 'Who do you think you are? You think the road belongs to you?' he shouts in impudence. 'Listen old man, get a move on now! I have been more than patient!' he remarks as dad appears near his car.

Pushpendra is now really angry. He just about controls his temper, not wanting to create a scene.

'Listen, young man. Show some respect. That's a veteran you are talking to.'

The driver remains defiant.

'Must have been a veteran, so what? You guys just haven't seen the world. You remain in your own cocoons. Look around man, smell the coffee. This is the real world.'

Suddenly there is pin drop silence. Pushpendra is embarrassed by the disrespect shown to his brother. The young driver doesn't realize he's touched a raw nerve.

Something snaps in my father. He is in the process of fastening his seat belt when he stops what he is doing. He opens the door and walks out. Mama is worried as to where he is headed. 'Hold on—where are you going?' she asks.

He just carries on walking towards the honking car. The driver has returned to his seat. He knocks on the window.

The irritated driver lowers his power window, 'Yes budhau, what do you want?'

My father just catches him by the collar and drags him straight out of the window. Despite his age his muscles haven't weakened. He starts choking him with his vice-like grip. The driver is helpless; he tries his best to free himself. No matter what he does my father's grip is firm. The man's face is losing colour. His wife realizes the danger.

'Please leave him, sir, I apologize on his behalf. Please, sir,' she begs.

My father ignores her. The driver's life seems to be ebbing. Pushpendra, Manu and my mother yell.

'What are you doing? He will die!'

He doesn't seem to hear them. Pushpendra runs out of his car.

'Dada! Stop for God's sake. He is about to die.'

'About to die…'

The words register somewhere in my father's mind. He releases his grip. The driver falls on the ground, almost lifeless, gasping for breath. His wife rushes to him.

Papa walks slowly towards Pushpendra's car, takes his seat. They leave for their destination, all of them absolutely quiet.

After a short drive they reach the memorial. All of them alight and pay their respects to the fallen soldiers at the memorial. Dad salutes silently and walks towards the car. He still looks troubled and distracted. Pushpendra starts the car. They are on the way home.

'Pushi,' Dad says.

'Yes, dada,' he replies.

'You remember what papa said to me when I was commissioned?'

'Yes, dada. Something to the effect that he could bear your loss, but not disgrace.'

'Yes, you are right,' my father acknowledges. He is quiet again, lost in his thoughts, recounting the words of the impertinent young driver.

'We haven't seen the world, he says! The bloody chap!' he mumbles, barely audible. 'You know, Pushi, sometimes I think I would have been better off dead, don't you think?'

Some questions are best left unanswered.

Postscript

It has been extremely difficult for me to get this factual account from my father. A testament not only to his humility but also to the sad memories of the loss of many of his comrades at arms. While I wrote this book my father insisted that it was not to be a biography. However, I do feel that some readers would like to know what happened in the family since the events narrated in this book. This postscript is for them.

My father has always been a quiet man. Socially, you would hardly feel his presence in a conversation or a gathering. In fact you could almost miss him—but for his very strong physical appearance.

Given his reticence whether the war affected him or not is hard to gauge. However, it is my conviction that still waters run deep. In my father's silence rests the wisdom of a man who has seen more in life than an average human being is likely to see.

Life for my father in the army never remained the same. His career was not exceptional. His injured hand did not allow prolonged written work, absolutely essential to do well on professional courses. Like any war veteran he would irritate instructors or colleagues while shooting down their grandiose but impractical plans. He knew they looked good only on large map boards. He had seen and experienced too much.

Only a very few senior officers could unmask his professional qualities. Blessed with an instinctive, God-given feel of terrain and abundant practical knowledge, his advice was invaluable in executing realistic plans. Only those who could discern these qualities benefited while interacting with him. It was his good fortune that some of these officers who recognized his strengths were on his promotion board when he was being considered for promotion. The fact that he was cleared for the rank of brigadier is to their credit. Personally he had resigned himself to going home quietly as a colonel.

Physically he remained absolutely fit, except for his hand which didn't really improve. Unable to close his wrist his hand actually became stone-like.

Time, it is said, is a natural healer and that was true for my father as well. He gradually healed. Mostly calm, he seldom lost his temper. On the rare occasions that he did lose his temper the trigger was hard to predict. It could be an innocuous truck driver lost in his thoughts, not allowing papa's car to overtake, or a snide remark by a stranger. When he did lose his temper, he would tremble with anger and could even be very physical, thrashing the daylights out of the person that had roused his anger. As family, we would be very embarrassed with his sudden outbursts and would even sympathize with the unfortunate person.

War takes a heavy toll on the families of those participating in the war too. My family has been no different.

The war had a permanent effect on my mother's personality. On 16 December 1971 she received a telephone call informing her that her husband was missing in action and presumed dead. The status remained the same for almost forty-five days until early February '72, when she finally received confirmation that her husband was alive. The uncertainty of those few months affected my mother adversely. She lost part of her gregarious nature and turned somewhat circumspect. From a lively, light-hearted person she took to religion and today routinely spends many hours in prayer. Asthma and related ailments got the better of an otherwise healthy, robust woman.

The reasons for such a dramatic change in her personality are not hard to find. In Rajput families (especially back then), the life of a widow was extremely difficult and they had little to look forward to. Considered inauspicious, they were resigned to spending the rest of their lives in the background, not to be seen or heard. To a young vivacious mother of two the prospect of spending the rest of her life as a widow would have been extremely intimidating. Though the news of her husband being alive and well came as a miraculous blessing, it did leave a scar on her psyche.

Barely six years old when the war commenced, I have very few memories of this difficult period. Miraculously, being part of a loving joint family, my mother managed to insulate my brother and I from what was happening in her life. For us things seemed normal.

Immediately on return from his ordeal my father decided to pack off both his sons to a boarding school. We joined Lawrence School, Lovedale, one of the best schools of the time. The school did us good as we lived a wonderful, happy and fulfilling life at Lovedale. What both of us have achieved in life is largely because of the upbringing we got and the school contributed to it in no small measure.

With the then meagre army salary my parents struggled to make ends meet. With no extra source of income money was hard to come by. They managed somehow. I don't recall seeing my parents ever buying anything expensive for themselves or indulging in small pleasures. That they lived in small towns like Jasai, Barmer or Bikaner in the '70s helped. Even if you wanted to there was no place to spend money.

With the award of the VrC to my father he received from the Rajasthan government approximately sixteen acres of agricultural land and from the Central government a railway pass which permitted free travel for a helper and himself in trains.

The land allotted to him by the government, though excellent, was in a remote corner of the desert. Just prior to his retirement he disposed of the same and bought some virgin land near Chhattargarh, Rajasthan. When he finally hung up his uniform he headed to Chhattargarh to commence farming. He left for the desert with nothing except a Maruti Gypsy,[47] which carried his meagre belongings. He lived off his Gypsy, toiling day and night in an attempt to make some headway in his new venture. He stayed alone, as he felt the hostile desert conditions were not suitable for my mother.

In about a year's time he had set up a rudimentary hut and had made some headway farming. My mother joined him and together they spent ten years setting up a decent farm and base at Chhattargarh. It was now developed sufficiently to interest locals into seeking it for annual contracts.

Meanwhile my brother and I were busy with our careers and our families. It was then that my parents made use of the Awardee Railway Pass visiting us and their grandchildren. They were present during each important milestone in the lives of their grandchildren. While writing this story, the fourth generation, my brother Vikram and I, are serving major generals in the Indian Army, while the fifth generation trains in the Academy.

Today my parents are resigned to a very easy pace of life at Jaipur. My father is generally out golfing every morning while my mother keeps the home running. Family get-togethers are common and regular.

As I mentioned in the preface each incident mentioned in the book is true, as my father saw and experienced. It is testimony to his humility that he quietly bore the pain and mental turmoil alone. I can vouch for the fact that no single person, including family, is aware of the entire truth. The book may surprise them too.

I was lucky to stumble upon the manuscript copies of my father's battle reports early in life. As children, only on one occasion, lying awake under the stars in Jasai,[48] were we able to coerce the account of the battle out of him. A few years back my niece Aishwarya was kind enough to spend many days recording his experiences for posterity. Later I requested her to do the same for my mother—I needed to get her side too. The memories of the events narrated by my father, audio recordings provided by Aishwarya and manuscript copies of my father's reports have provided the material in writing this book.

~

While reading about the Battle of Daruchhian you may wonder—how could things go so horribly wrong?

For the attackers one could easily attribute it to an inexplicable run of bad luck—leading officers/JCOs accidentally stepping on mines, being struck in the first burst of fire or simply losing their lives to artillery fire. If things had gone his way Lt Col Inderjit could well have been a hero.

Conversely, if press reports are to be believed, the providence that brought the commanding officer of the enemy battalion defending the sector to Daruchhian on an inspection—just in time to coordinate the battle—worked in favour of the defenders. The company commander himself did a commendable job defending his position against all odds, earning him a gallantry award as per reports in the Pakistani media.

But it would be foolish to blame the failure of the attack on luck alone. When dealing with human lives one needs to ensure that military plans do not ride on the need to be lucky.

The fact that eight officers, seven JCOs and 149 men of other ranks were killed, injured or went missing in battle is extraordinary and deserves introspection.

The commanding officer's plan was unconventional and suffered from *'over ambitiousness'*[49] and *'a lack of regard of the enemy's capabilities'*.[50] Even as you read this book, in some remote corner of our country, soldiers are executing some unconventional plan or the other for their COs. The Battle of Daruchhian has a lesson for those who plan such operations, as well as those who approve them.

There were some major flaws in the plan which resulted in its failure and the extraordinary casualties at Daruchhian.

Firstly, the attack plan was *'ill planned'* and *'the wisdom of launching it from several divergent axes [was] questionable'*.[51]

As the military historian Maj Gen Sukhwant Singh explains:

> Each prong was independent of the others, with its own reserves, making its own entry to the obstacle, suffering its own casualties and fending for itself in case of failure.

As it happened, the prongs bogged down in the minefield and suffered such heavy casualties, especially in leadership that the attack petered out, except in the case of the company working its way along the West Spur. There was now a chance to exploit the successful entry into the enemy locality from that side, but the battalion commander and his reserves fell behind in terms of time to exploit this limited success to advantage. Even if he had started for the West Spur immediately, he would have reached it after about three hours or so, and by that time the enemy would have readjusted his weapons. In any event, day would have broken by then, and as it happened the movement was caught in observed fire.

It would perhaps have been profitable to contain the locality from the east and develop the attack along the West/South West spurs, with the battalion commander and his reserves located at a central place close behind or in between the Spurs, ready to reinforce success, whenever achieved, on either prong.

In case of hesitancy or slow progress, the battalion commander should have been able to get things moving by personal command in battle. As it was, he was almost left out of it, content to command by telephone or radio. Moreover, strengthening close thrust would have been better for concentration of artillery and infantry resources, as also for tighter battle control.[52]

However, '*the Commanding Officer alone cannot be blamed for this—the plan had the approval of the Brigade as well as the Divisional Commanders*'.[53] If the plan was not tactically sound how and why had the brigade and divisional commanders allowed its execution?

Another major flaw in the plan was inadequate reconnaissance of the objective.

The defended localities on the main picquet along the Ceasefire Line had their defence potential enhanced over almost a quarter of a century by methodical laying of mines, erection of other obstacles like wire, and construction of shell proof fortifications and bunkers with weapons sweeping the slopes with murderous fire.[54]

A few days of reconnaissance to the battalion, as requested by Inderjit, would have revealed the same. Why then was the battalion launched in a hurry?

The artillery fire plan for the battle was extremely complicated given the need to support multi-directional attacks in mountainous terrain. It required exceptional coordination which in the limited time was impossible. The technical aspects seemed to have been glossed over.

As it is, many soldiers lost their lives on the enemy obstacles and minefields. Those lucky enough to get past were subjected to relentless artillery fire. What the helpless soldiers didn't realize was that they were facing the brunt of fire not only of their enemy, but Indian guns as well. A large number of casualties on the night of 13/14 December were attributed to artillery.

Thankfully neither my father nor his colleagues have had to bear the burden of the flaws in the plan or why and by whom the plans were cleared. They just followed orders, ignoring the anger and frustration that they may have felt during various stages of the battle. My father was honoured to fight alongside such gallant comrades, many of whom lost their lives that fateful night. His message to them—'*Rest in peace, dear comrades. We shall meet again!*' It is nearly fifty years since. Understandably he can scarcely speak about the events without getting emotional.

~

I have been permitted to write this book only on the condition that most part of the returns (if any!) from this book are utilized towards looking after the martyrs of Daruchhian or their kin. This I promise to do.

As my father crosses the magical age of 82, I think he's healed enough to share his account of the battle. He owed it to his comrades in arms and the future generations of The Grenadiers.

It is also a fact that my father is alive today due to the honourable actions of some of the Pakistani officers and men and women who my father was fortunate to have encountered.

Of special mention is the Pakistani major who prevented his colleagues from killing my grievously wounded father as well as Colonel Mehmood Hassan and other medical staff who treated him in the various Pakistani medical establishments. Warfare is a nasty business, but to show humanity during testing times is in accordance with the highest code of conduct of a soldier. On behalf of my family I convey our gratitude to those unknown soldiers.

Brigadier (Retd) Hamir Singh being felicitated at a function in Jaipur in his old age.

My sincere thanks to the Rajasthan government for re-including his name in the list of invitees for the Governor's 'At Home', which he makes it a point to attend every year.

To us, his family, this account of the battle will remain an inspiration. As my son Veer Vaibhav Singh Rathore trains to become a fifth-generation officer I am confident that the book will always remind him of his proud ancestral legacy.

Finally, as I mentioned in my dedication, it will take us many rebirths to reciprocate our gratitude to our parents. We are truly blessed!

Jai Hind!

Glossary and Explanations

Terms Relating to the Military

citation: A citation for a gallantry award is a brief written description of a courageous act for which the soldier is recommended for an award. The citation is written by a person who has witnessed the act, generally the commanding officer. An independent body then verifies the action. If the facts are found to be true the person being cited is awarded the gallantry award.

epaulet: A shoulder piece indicating rank worn on the coat or jacket of a military uniform.

FUP: An acronym for Forming-Up Place. It is a pre-designated area in which troops assemble in preparation for an operation.

Havildar: Sergeant.

Havildar Major: Company Havildar Major (CHM) is the most senior non-commissioned officer in a company, equivalent to a company sergeant major.

JCO: An acronym for Junior Commissioned Officer, a military rank of the Indian Army, higher than Havildar (sergeant) and lower than Lieutenant.

NCO: A non-commissioned officer (NCO) is a military officer who has not earned a commission. Their position of authority is by promotion through the enlisted ranks. In the Indian Army soldiers from the rank of Lance Naik (Lance Corporal) to Havildar (Sergeant) are called NCOs.

OC: Till the '70s the term OC (Officer Commanding) was widely used in the Indian Army for Lieutenant Colonel rank officers commanding battalions/regiments. Today, command is generally at Colonel rank and the commonly used term is either CO (commanding officer) or Commandant (in armoured regiments).

pillbox: A pillbox is a small reinforced bunker, normally equipped with loopholes through which weapons are fired. It is hardened to protect against small arms fire and grenades.

radio operator: A radio operator (also, formerly, wireless operator) is a person who is responsible for the operations of the military radio set and equipment.

RV: RV or rendezvous is a military term for a previously designated place during an operation.

sahab: A term used in the Indian Army to address or to refer to an officer or JCO.

Sowar: Meaning 'the one who rides' or 'rider' was the lowest military rank of soldiers in the Indian cavalry. The rank is still used in the Indian armoured corps.

Subedar: A JCO rank of the Indian Army, senior to the rank of Havildar.

Subedar Major: Subedar Major (SM) is the seniormost rank among junior commissioned officers in the Indian Army. Having risen to the highest rank in his line, the Subedar Major occupies a pivotal position in the battalion. He commands respect from all and is the main adviser to the commanding officer (CO). His role is all encompassing and he keeps a 'feel' of the battalion's pulse.

Vir Chakra (VrC): An Indian gallantry award presented for acts of gallantry in the presence of the enemy on the battlefield.

Units of the Army (both Indian and Pakistani)

14 Grenadiers: An infantry battalion of the Grenadiers Regiment of the Indian Army.

16 Cavalry: A renowned erstwhile cavalry (now armoured) regiment of the Indian Army.

196 Mountain Regiment: An artillery regiment of the Indian Army.

2 Grenadiers: An infantry battalion of the Indian Army.

2 Indian Field Regiment: A renowned artillery regiment of the Indian Army.

3/9 GR: 3rd Battalion of the 9 Gorkha Regiment is an Indian infantry battalion.

45 Cavalry: An armoured regiment of the Indian Army.

6/11 GR: 6th Battalion of the 11 Gorkha Rifles is an infantry battalion of the Indian Army.

7 Mahar: An infantry battalion of the Indian Army.

Glossary and Explanations

8 Cavalry: An armoured regiment of the Indian Army.

Azad Kashmir Battalion: The Azad Kashmir Regiment, also written as AK Regt, is one of the six infantry regiments of the Pakistan Army. Its battalions are referred to as POK (Pakistan Occupied Kashmir) Battalion in India.

CMP: Corps of Military Police.

Ganga Risala: 'Risala' is an Urdu word which means mounted cavalry. Ganga Risala, a camel cavalry regiment, was founded by Maharaja Ganga Singh of Bikaner, India in the year 1889. It was also known as Bikaner Camel Corps. The regiment now exists as 13 Grenadiers, an infantry battalion of the Indian Army.

National Cadet Corps (NCC): The National Cadet Corps is the youth wing of the Armed Forces. It is open to school and college students on a voluntary basis. The cadets are given basic military training in small arms and parades.

Poona Horse: A renowned erstwhile cavalry (now armoured) regiment of the Indian Army.

Rajputana Rifles: An infantry regiment of the Indian Army.

RAP: The Regimental Aid Post (RAP) is a front-line military medical establishment incorporated into an infantry battalion or armoured regiment for the immediate treatment and triage of battlefield casualties.

General Terms

'Ram Ram': A form of greeting.
baba: Wise old man.
bai: A Rajasthani term for daughter.
baisa: A Rajasthani word for 'Miss'.
banna: A Rajasthani word for young Rajput boys.
bara khana: Literally, 'big food'; a term used for a special meal.
baraat: A groom's wedding procession in north India.
bausa: A Rajasthani term for mother.
beta: The Hindi word for son; used in some contexts to simply mean child as well.
bhabhi: A word for the elder brother's wife used in north India.
bhajans: Religious hymns.
budhau: A Hindi slang for an old man.
chakor: The chakor is a type of partridge found in the inner ranges of western Himalayas. A game bird, it has a light-brown back while its breast is grey in colour.

chhang: A very popular local beer-like brew, chhang is relished in the Himalayas around Sikkim, Tibet and Nepal. Barley, millet (finger-millet) or rice grains are used to brew the drink.

dada: A Rajasthani term for elder brother.

dal: A general term used in the Indian subcontinent for lentils and the also the stew made by cooking them.

dholak: A two-headed hand-drum from the Indian subcontinent.

Diwali: The Hindu festival of lights.

Dogras: An ethno-linguistic group of north India consisting of speakers of the Dogri language. They live mainly in the Jammu region and in adjoining areas of Punjab and Himachal Pradesh.

Gaon Burha: Gaon Burha literally means 'eldest man of the village'. Considered the wise man of the village he is accorded respect and in some regions even enjoys administrative powers in matters of the village.

ghazal: A poem or an ode originating in Arabic poetry, now common in many regions in South Asia, that has as its theme the pain of loss or separation or unrequited love.

gurdwara: A place of assembly and worship for Sikhs.

halal: Halal food essentially refers to food that adheres to Islamic law; more commonly used to refer to the prescribed Islamic form of slaughtering animals or poultry and the meat obtained therefrom.

harmonium: An Indian musical instrument; a reed organ.

haud: A small outdoor water tank or reservoir for irrigation purposes.

haveli: A traditional house in the Indian subcontinent generally built around a courtyard.

iftar: The evening meal with which Muslims end their daily Ramadan fast at sunset.

jalebis: An Indian sweet snack made by deep-frying white flour batter in a criss-crossing pattern but roughly circular shapes and then soaked in sugar syrup.

jawaisa: A Rajasthani term for son-in-law.

jija: A Rajasthani term for elder sister.

juley: An all-purpose Ladakhi word which may mean a salutation, hello, goodbye, good morning, good night, please, thank you, etc.

Kaimkhani Muslims: A Muslim Rajput community of India. They are said to have descended from Chauhan Rajputs, who in the 14th century converted from Hinduism to Islam during the reign of Firoz Shah Tughlaq.

Glossary and Explanations 231

kanwarsa: The male member of the Rajput family whose father is alive is addressed as 'kanwar'; the suffix '-sa' is added in respect. In traditional families children would generally address their father as kanwarsa.

kirtan: A genre of religious performance art which involves narrating, reciting, telling, describing a legend, or expressing loving devotion to a deity, or discussing spiritual ideas.

Krishna: A major deity in Hinduism. He is worshipped as the eighth avatar of the god Vishnu and also as the supreme God in his own right.

kurta: A loose collarless shirt worn in many regions of South Asia.

mandir: A Hindu temple.

Mertia Rathore: A martial clan of Rajputs, Mertia Rathores originated from a place called Merta in Rajasthan, India.

miyan: An Urdu word for gentleman.

muddha: A cane chair.

nala: A Hindi word for a stream of water; a rivulet or brook.

Nehru coat: A closed-neck coat, made popular by a former Indian prime minister, Jawaharlal Nehru.

paratha: A layered flatbread common throughout the Indian subcontinent; whether made with or without a stuffing, ghee or clarified butter is a primary ingredient which gives it its richness and sets it apart from its staple flatbread cousin, chapati.

pehelwan: Wrestler.

PT: Physical training.

qawwali: A form of Sufi Islamic devotional singing, originating in the Indian subcontinent.

qawwals: Qawwali singers.

ragini: Classical folk music of Haryana (as used in this book).

Rajput: A martial community of India historically associated with warriorhood.

saafa: A Rajput turban.

salwar: A pair of trousers.

samosa: A deep-fried snack with a spiced filling usually made with potatoes.

saree: A women's garment from the Indian subcontinent that consists of an unstitched drape.

shehnai: A wind instrument from the Indian subcontinent; widely used during marriages, processions, and religious festivities.

thali: A round platter used to serve food.

yaar: A common Indian word for friend.

Notes

1. A hill feature on the Pakistan side of the Line of Control between India and Pakistan.
2. See the official website for gallantry awards of the Ministry of Defence, Government of India: https://gallantryawards.gov.in/Awardee/hamir-singh
3. Inderjit Singh, *Daruchhian: A Saga of Valour*, KW Publishers Pvt Ltd, 2016.
4. Gautam Sharma, *Valour and Sacrifice: Famous Regiments of the Indian Army*, South Asia Books, 1990, p. 93.
5. Citation of IC 18321 Captain Jagdish Chander Gosain, VrC (Posthumous): On the night of 13/14 December 1971, Jagdish Chander Gosain was detailed as the forward observation officer with a leading company in the attack on an enemy defended area in the Western Sector. The attack was held up due to effective fire from a few cement concrete bunkers. Jagdish Chander Gosain therefore arranged to fire his guns in direct firing role on the bunkers by directly exposing himself in the lethal zone of own shells as well as that of the enemy. Immediately after the air strike, the officer assumed command of the company and assaulted the bunkers in broad daylight along with 40 other ranks. In this action Jagdish Chander Gosain displayed gallantry, leadership, determination and made the supreme sacrifice for the call of duty in keeping with the best traditions of the Indian Army.
6. It is a mandatory military course for Indian Army officers of Major/Lieutenant Colonel rank prior to assuming command of their battalions/regiments. It is conducted at the Army War College, Mhow, near Indore, Madhya Pradesh.
7. A village in the Poonch district of Jammu and Kashmir, India.

8   A hill feature near the LOC near Poonch.
9   Singh, *Daruchhian*, p. 34.
10 Ibid.
11 A village in the Poonch district of Jammu and Kashmir, India.
12 See S.N. Prasad et al., eds., *History of the 1971 India Pakistan War*, New Delhi: History Division, Ministry of Defence, Government of India, 1992, p. 322 (available online at https://www.bharat-rakshak.com/ARMY/history/1971war/280-war-history-1971.html, last accessed 20 August 2021).
13 During the Battle of Chittaur, forces led by the Mughal Emperor Akbar surrounded and besieged 8,000 Rajputs and around 40,000 peasants under the command of Jaimal in Chittorgarh, India.
14 The essence of this saying is that you need to adapt to the place you live in—a similar sentiment as 'When in Rome, do as the Romans do!'
15 'My Time as a PoW in Pakistan-a story of courage, pain, pride and hope | Capt. GR CHOUDHARY | TEDxRTU' (available online at https://www.youtube.com/watch?v=yZd-tCw5_GI, last accessed 20 August 2021).
16 A city in Rajasthan, India.
17 Refers to Hamir. In traditional Rajasthani families wives would avoid calling their husband's by their name.
18 Company Havildar Majors are also called Havildar Major.
19 Fictitious name. My father is unable to recollect his actual name.
20 Fictitious name. My father is unable to recollect his actual name.
21 Fictitious name used as my father is unable to recollect the ICRC official's actual name.
22 Fictitious name. My father is unable to recollect his actual name.
23 My father is reasonably sure the officer belonged to 12 Cavalry of the Pakistan Army.
24 3 Battalion of 9 Gorkha Regiment.
25 A town in Himachal Pradesh, India.
26 Kitchener College was founded in 1929 at Nowgong, Chhatarpur, Madhya Pradesh, India to train soldiers from the regular army, navy and air force for commission as

officers in the Indian Army. Today it is known as the Army Cadet College and is located in the same premises as the Indian Military Academy, Dehradun.

27. Gurdeep Singh Kler, *Unsung Battles of 1962*, Lancer Publishers, 1995, p. 226.

28. Citation of IC 403 Brigadier Kalyan Singh, VSM Class 1 (now changed to PVSM): Brigadier Kalyan Singh was enlisted in the Army in 1933 and was commissioned in 1940. He saw active service in North Africa during World War II and was taken prisoner of war. He has held various staff and command appointments, including those of Officer Commanding a Field Regiment, Chief Instructor, School of Artillery and Deputy Director Artillery at Army Headquarters, before he was posted as Commander of an Artillery Brigade in August 1961. (He attended the Long Gunnery Staff Course [Coast Artillery] in the United Kingdom in May 1956.) In October 1962, when the Chinese forces developed a threat to Tawang in overwhelming numbers and from various directions, it was considered that our troops could not hold out for long against the heavy odds. It was decided to carry out a planned withdrawal from Tawang and to delay the enemy north of Se La for some time, so that our troops could build up a position at Se La. Brigadier Kalyan Singh accomplished this task in a masterly manner in the face of heavy enemy pressure. He displayed courage and military skill of a very high order.

29. Fictitious name. My father is unable to recall the actual name.

30. It is mentioned on page 321, in Chapter 8, 'Pakistan Chooses War: Operations in J&K', *History of the 1971 India Pakistan War*, that Lt Col Nazir Ahmed Khan, CO, 26 AK Battalion was killed at Thanpir along with his battery commander. My father, however, cannot recollect the exact name or whether he is the same person mentioned in the incident.

31. Fictitious house number. My father is unable to recollect the actual number of the bungalow on Mall Road.

32. A Bangladeshi playback singer and composer. She is one of the best-known singers in South Asia.

33. Lyallpur, now known as Faisalabad, is the third-most-populous city in Pakistan.

34 A. Anil Athale, 'My days as a prisoner of war in Pakistan', *Rediff.com*, 27 February 2019 (https://www.rediff.com/news/special/my-days-as-a-prisoner-of-war-in-pakistan/20161216.htm, last accessed 20 August 2021).

35 Faith Johnston, *Four Miles from Freedom: Escape from a Pakistani POW Camp*, Random House India, 2013, p. 54.

36 A geographical region in north-central India. It lies along the Chambal and Yamuna River valleys, in south-eastern Rajasthan, south-western Uttar Pradesh and northern Madhya Pradesh.

37 An American luxury automobile marque built by the Packard Motor Car Company of Detroit, Michigan, United States.

38 A town in Sagar district in the state of Madhya Pradesh, India.

39 Many of our soldiers, believed to be POWs in Pakistan, were never repatriated. Even after nearly five decades since the 1971 war there is still no clarity over their numbers and fate. Our government has officially acknowledged that 54 soldiers and officers of the Indian armed forces are missing or were killed in action during the 1971 war. Even today there is a section of people, especially family members, that believe that many of the missing POWs are alive and remain imprisoned in different jails in Pakistan.

40 Sukhwant Singh, *Defence of India's Western Border*, vol. 2 of *India's Wars Since Independence*, Lancer Publishers, 2013, p. 58.

41 Ibid.

42 Gautam Das, *Unlearned Lessons: An Appraisal of India's Military Mishaps*, Har Anand Publications, 2007, p. 224.

43 A village near Lahore located in Punjab, Pakistan where the border crossing between India and Pakistan takes place.

44 Patriotic slogans meaning 'Victory to Mother India' and 'Mother, I bow to thee'.

45 A brand of fruit-flavoured carbonated soft drinks.

46 Fictitious name. My father is unable to recollect his actual name.

47 A four-wheel-drive vehicle based on the long wheelbase Suzuki Jimny.

48 A small army cantonment near Barmer, Rajasthan.

49 Das, *Unlearned Lessons*, p. 224.
50 Ibid.
51 Prasad et al., *History of the 1971 India Pakistan War*, p. 325.
52 Singh, *Defence of India's Western Border*, pp. 57–58.
53 Prasad et al., *History of the 1971 India Pakistan War*, p. 325.
54 Singh, *Defence of India's Western Border*, p. 57.

Acknowledgments

I am indebted to my loving wife Vaishali for pushing me to put pen to paper, and bearing the boredom patiently while I was engrossed in this project.

My daughter Vaishnavi and son Veer Vaibhav Singh Rathore, the special bond that you share with your grandparents inspired me to tell their story.

Vaishali and Vaishnavi, you were not only the first editors of the book but also provided me with an honest critique after each draft, and there were several drafts.

My brother Vikram, who has always looked out for me, thanks for representing our father proudly in The Grenadiers. Vikram painstakingly went through each word of this book with my father to ensure the accuracy of the contents. A special thanks to his wife Shalini and children Aishwarya and Rajanya Singh for recording my father's narration, an extremely important part of this project.

My sincere gratitude to my father-in-law, Lieutenant General Y.S. Tomar, PVSM, the reason my father joined The Grenadiers, for being his inspirational instructor at the Indian Military Academy.

I would like to place on record my sincere thanks to all others who contributed to help me complete the project.